D1461636

HERITAGE OF THE KAISER'S CHILDREN

RUTH MICHAELIS-JENA

HERITAGE OF THE KAISER'S CHILDREN

an autobiography

CANONGATE
1983

First published in 1983
by Canongate Publishing Ltd,
17 Jeffrey Street, Edinburgh
Scotland

ISBN 0 86241 046 0

*The publishers acknowledge
the financial assistance of the
Scottish Arts Council in the
publication of this volume.*

Typeset in 11/13pt Bembo by
Witwell Limited., Liverpool

*Printed in Great Britain by Robert Hartnoll Ltd.
Bodmin, Cornwall.*

contents

PART I

Childhood in Ruritania

Chapter 1

The kaleidoscope of memory has become brighter since the old house has gone. I harboured a death wish for the house of my childhood ever since I had to leave it hurriedly on a dark morning so many years ago. I was jealous of others who might live in it, possess it as if I had never been.

I saw the house again once, war-scarred and a semi-ruin, and I felt strangely relieved. It would never again be as I had known it, it would have to be re-built, it would change, it might even have to be pulled down.

And pulled down it was.

Then the past began to haunt me: our house, its every corner, at different seasons, on different days. I could hear its sounds, I could smell its smells. It all lived again, it belonged to me. No intruders now. It compelled me to come to it.

There was the large dining-room on the ground floor, with its window looking out on the busy main street. There was the scent of hyacinth, blue hyacinths in long-stemmed glasses, at the turn of the year, in early February on my mother's birthday. Blue was her favourite colour. The linoleum on the drawing-room floor was blue, a vast sea to float boats on, and seat the dolls by in their deck-chairs.

There was Father's study, book-lined, and a bright yellow canary twittering in a wicker cage.

In this study, sitting at his desk, nervously turning a pencil in his hand, a gesture I came to know so well later on, he was waiting one October night in the year of our Lord 1905, made eerie through an untimely fall of snow. He was waiting for what seemed an eternity to him.

When the family doctor opened the door at midnight, Father complained about an infernal cat miaowing.

"The cat miaowing is your daughter," said the doctor, "Congratulations!"

A few minutes earlier he had bent over a young woman, lying pale and exhausted in a bedroom on the second floor. He had answered an unspoken question in her half-open eyes.

"This time it's a gipsy, small but strong. She will live all right."

And my mother had closed her eyes, smiling vaguely. Some eighteen months before she had buried her first child, also a girl, only a few days old.

Her second one, brown-skinned, hazel-eyed, her head covered in black curls, now lay in the pink-curtained cradle, asleep and safe.

Not for many months to come did my mother really believe me safe. The horror of seeing her first child fall into convulsions and die, had left her with an obsession. It would happen again. Only much later when her own mother who had brought up a row of children, reassured her, did I become real to her. She stopped waking in the middle of the night to rush to the cradle, and see whether I was still there, or peep anxiously through the curtains in the daytime.

I had come to stay, it seemed.

I was born into the bourgeois comfort of a small German town, Detmold, capital of Lippe, one of those minute principalities which survived the French Revolution and the wars that followed. There were records of an early settlement close to the place where the Roman legions suffered defeat at the hands of Arminius, chief of the Cherusci tribe. Detmold became a town in the fourteenth century, and grew under the protection of knights and noblemen who eventually rose to the status of ruling princes. The hefty round tower of the castle stood, a reminder of former stronghold days. Half of the moat had been filled in to make a park in the 'English' manner, carp rose in the water of the other half, which, frozen over, provided a fine skating-rink in winter. The old town with its narrow crooked lanes, and its streets of high-gabled houses had long since burst its walls. Many of the houses remained as they had been for centuries, their oak beams decorated with the initials of owners long since gone, with ornate scrolls and perhaps a proverb or quotation from the Scriptures. Big brass handles shone on the heavy carved doors. Broad thoroughfares made up the New Town, with handsome establishments designed in the eighteenth and nineteenth centuries for the gentry and the rising middle class. The waters of small streams had been tamed to form a canal by a ruler who, like other German princelings, wished his residence to become a minor Versailles. His scheme was designed to connect the old fortified town castle with a new country pleasance laid out elegantly on a wooded site with terraces, conservatories and a banqueting hall, waterfalls, statues andd belvederes. The court was conveyed in gondolas from one place to the other without ever having to set foot on dusty streets or muddy roads. The splendour was to last a mere twenty years or so. Then, during a glittering feast, the decorations caught fire and the whole went up in flames. What remained of the frivolities was turned into a gloomy family mausoleum by a more sober princely descendant. The canal was still there, and with limes planted alongside, it became the setting for a fashionable *Allee*, a place for strolling, where ladies and gentlemen could take the air with decorum.

What had been a cemetery around an ancient church in the heart of the old town was now a market place. Along it ran the main street which had at one time connected two of the town's gates.

It was here that I entered the world.

The court with its own army, protecting a country not larger than a couple of biggish estates, had for many years given the town a certain lustre and its inhabitants an illusion of grandeur. Gossip about 'the court' was a favourite topic of conversation, with balls, hunts, parades and the reception of foreign princes ranking high. Every shopkeeper, every artisan aspired to be 'appointed to the court', to be able to put a coat of arms above his door, and be called *Herr Hoflieferant*. Industries were few: some old-established printing works, a biscuit factory or two, and furniture-making, helped by plentiful supplies of timber from the surrounding woodlands. Brick-makers were a special class of workmen, looking after their own small crofts in the winter, leaving every spring to follow their trade in places as far afield as Holland, while their womenfolk minded the crofts, a cow or two and a couple of goats. In the autumn the men returned, their pockets jingling with silver.

A small world which seemed secure, with everything foreseeable and hence planned. Even an infant's first outing was not left to chance.

All through a long cold winter I was kept indoors so that no harsh wind or flurry of snow might harm me. With the first rays of a warmer sun my mother naturally wanted to show me off, but the family doctor had to be consulted beforehand. Only he could decide on the proper moment. After measuring the temperature in his garden for a few days running, he pronounced the weather fit, and April saw my first outing.

My earliest and quite vivid recollection is nightmarish. There is an upturned pram and myself rolling down an embankment, screaming. Then, the face of an old man who lifted me into his arms and put a rose into my hand. I can now recall distinctly the feeling of comfort and security after a bad shock. I was told later that a young nurse-maid had taken me out one afternoon when she met other maids, and stopped, chatting and gesturing. As she lifted her hand for a moment off the pram handle, the whole thing left the path, ran down the banks of the canal, and overturned. I fell out and trundled to the water's edge. There were shrieks from the maids and passers-by went to the rescue. An old man picked up the miserable bundle, and in his nearby garden pulled me that rose. No lasting harm came to me, but I often wonder whether the claustrophobia I experience in tunnels and darkened rooms, has its origin in the dim memory of the upturned pram.

Next I remember travelling, a journey by train when I was not quite two years old. We went to my mother's home some hundred miles away, and I recall the strange and enjoyable sensation of seeing houses, trees, fields, and a great number of black-and-white cows swishing past. Then came trouble. On the way to the dining-car I saw the harmonica-like fittings joining the carriages, and they terrified me. I would not eat, I would not play, I cried for the rest of the journey, shouting: 'The train is *kaputt*, it's broken; I want to go home.' New surroundings, new people soon made me forget the 'broken' train. During that holiday I even picked up enough courage to walk alone when until then I had been frightened to let go of my mother's hand. I also remember the excitement of being lifted up to a big kind of tube on the wall, and speaking into it to an aunt who lived a few streets away – my first encounter with the telephone.

When in time the journey home was talked about, I thought at once about the 'broken' train, and I firmly declared that I was not going on it. Eventually a favourite uncle appeased me by telling me that the old train had been thrown into the river, and that we were going on a brand-new one instead. On the journey they kept me away from the joints, and all was well. Two newly acquired treasures made me happy, one was a tiny shopping basket given me by my grandmother, the other a small piece of multi-coloured bunting. During our stay the university town of Marburg was gaily beflagged in the colours of the many student associations during their end-of-term festivities. I asked everybody to get a knife, and 'cut down a bit of flag' for me. And somehow this little piece had come into my possession. It stayed pinned up above my bed for years.

I must have been four or five years old when I accompanied my parents on their annual visit to a spa in the Harz mountains. My father took the waters every morning before breakfast, and I was his eager companion. From our hotel we walked along past some houses with neat little gardens, to a square surrounded by chestnut trees. There a band played, and people walked up and down, sipping their prescribed glasses of mineral water. I liked the music, and also, as it was June, I liked collecting the small green chestnuts which fall off the trees when the red and white candles of their blossoms have gone. Sometimes I played with a rubber ball, bouncing it or throwing it straight up into the air as high as I could. The ball was striped black, white and red, the German imperial colours, and carried the legend: *Unsere Zukunft liegt auf dem Wasser*, a saying appropriate to the navy-aspiring *Kaiser*, utterly unintelligible, yet fascinating to a child who asked to have it read to her. One morning my ball bounced into the grounds of a nearby villa and seemed gone for ever, but a lady soon came out of the gate and handed me back the ball. She was handsome with a lot of snow-white hair piled high on her head. My father made me curtsy and thank her. The lady, he said, was Russian, a relation of the Tzar who in Russia was something like our *Kaiser*. I was impressed. It was, I believe, the first time that I had met somebody from a far-off country. Walled towns were familiar to me – our own town had a small section of its ancient wall preserved – and I had come to think of foreign countries as large pieces of land surrounded by walls. I dearly longed to see such a wall, and peep into the country beyond. But I do not think I ever spoke to anybody about it.

My first continuous memory goes back to our house. I loved it. It had a life of its own, and I was sure it loved me too. Its pointed gable and broad comfortable front seemed to keep a friendly watch over me. The earliest mention of the house occurs in seventeenth-century records, though it was possibly built a hundred or more years before that. It was owned by generations of respectable townsfolk, several aldermen among them, and bought by my grandfather in 1862 to accommodate a growing family. My father, then five years old, had lived in it ever since.

The rooms of the house, some with heavily beamed ceilings, were low and on different levels, often reached by a few odd steps. There was a vast deep cellar down a flight of stone stairs behind a thick wooden door. Part of the cellar was shut off by another lighter door, pierced with airholes. Through them came a strange smell of wine and old wood. Father held the keys to this, and I would get an occasional glimpse of dust-covered bottles when I accompanied him to fetch some wine. Here father kept his favourite Tokay. It was the first wine I knew by name, and he allowed me to sip from his mid-morning glass now and again. The 'apple-cellar' was in the underground maze, too. Apples and pears, bought in quantity direct from the farm, were placed on airing-shelves in the autumn. Twice a week through the winter my mother went down, carrying a paraffin lamp, to inspect the fruit and any showing the slightest blemish would be collected for immediate use. It was quite an adventure to go down with Mother also to a deeper part of the cellar where the ground was soft sand, and where the winter root vegetables were kept, dug in, to be taken out when wanted. A pungent smell of leek and celeriac hung in the air. Several hundredweight of winter potatoes were stored in wooden bins. They were brought on a farm cart every October, one kind for mashing, another for cooking in their jackets, and yet another small firm variety for making potato salad. Potatoes were all known by their names, and I remember best 'little red mice', a name that intrigued me when I was sent to fetch a basketful.

At the top of the house were huge attics with an intricate pattern of heavy rafters and wooden beams, carrying the tiled roof. It was strictly forbidden to swing from the rafters at the sides where they sloped. I could touch them, and it gave me an odd sensation to do so. I went up with the maids in winter when the attics were used for drying the household linen carried up in large wicker baskets and hung on lines stretching from rafter to rafter. In one corner was a small secret place, mysteriously called 'the smoking chamber'. It was always locked, and to this day I conjure up it's rough wooden door when I think of the forbidden chamber in Bluebeard's castle. I eventually discovered that it was locked for no more sinister reason than to keep the soot from blowing about. Years ago the little room had been used for the smoking of hams and sausages, suspended from strong iron hooks over a wood-chip fire. An opening in the roof had allowed the smoke to get away, and this very hole might now allow soot to soil newly washed sheets and table cloths, hence the locked door.

In 1911, from these attics, I saw the first Zeppelin pass over the town . Its happy and innocent task was to throw a bunch of flowers for the director of the court theatre.

Our daily life was spent between cellar and attics. On the ground floor was 'the shop' – slightly remote from my existence – and behind it a small room where we breakfasted. It just held a round table, chairs and a serving board. On the other side was a large dining-room, used also as a sitting-room when remaining on the ground floor was convenient. My father's study-cum-office and the kitchen made up the rest. All the doors gave on to a big Dutch-tiled hall. Its blue-and-white tiles were constantly washed and polished and could be dangerously slippery, as I learnt to my dismay. I was sliding along one day while the maid was busy washing the floor, and landed straight in her bucket, legs in the air. I can still feel the horrible clamminess of my brown velvet dress complete with lace collar – a proud possession – now ruined for ever with the nasty lukewarm water.

Three drawing-rooms were on the first floor, old-fashioned and very comfortable. Some of their furniture had come with a bride of a generation or two ago and was still looked after lovingly. The rooms were small, but interconnecting doors, thrown open on special occasions, gave the whole of the first-floor elegance and spaciousness. On the same level at the back of the house were guest-rooms and a large bathroom, not a shining cubicle but a square room furnished with chests of drawers full of the softest towels, a large table, chairs and a big white enamel bath. A roaring stove, fired by coal, supplied plenty of hot water, and kept the room deliciously warm always. It was a place to linger in, and we did, particularly when my mother washed my very long thick hair. I hated the combing out, and could only be kept quiet by having stories told to me, an entertainment I never tired of in the cosy damp warmth of the bathroom.

Our bedrooms were on the second floor, so was the nursery and more guest-rooms. The floors were joined by broad sweeping stairs, hiding innumerable cupboards, wonderful to explore. Other small rooms were tucked away in odd corners: sleeping quarters for the maids, a tiny dark place called 'the shoe-cleaning room', a former dairy, now disused, where my sledge, toboggan, skates and rugs only in demand in winter, were stored. There was a wooden balcony at the back of the house on first floor level, overlooking a bare courtyard. What must have been a long narrow garden – they still existed in one part of the street – had been built on. Tacked on to the ground floor was 'the barn', a large solid building, the height of two storeys. It had contained stable and hayloft at a time when every well-established burgher kept a carriage and pair, and perhaps a cow or two. In my father's schooldays in the mid-sixties of the nineteenth century, cows grazed on the common through the day, and were driven back at night when they found their own sheds without difficulty. The cows disappeared from the scene only when they became dangerous obstacles to an electric tramway early installed by far-sighted city-fathers. In my day 'the barn' was used as a laundry, and coal and firewood were stored in the horse-boxes. The place had come down in the world, yet it still provided a magic playground.

Our house was not far from the castle where the ruling prince and his family lived. From my bedroom window I could see the red-and-yellow painted sentry-boxes, and the guards springing to attention when a member of the Household passed the gates. We were flanked by the *Hofbäcker* – the court baker – on one side, and the *Hofapotheker* – the court apothecary – on the other. The apothecary's was a fine old house, its front and gable rich with ornamental wooden beams. One bore a motto praising the value of herbs to suffering mankind. Prescriptions were made up in a back room where the apothecary could be seen busy with mortar and pestle. Most houses in our street were of lath-and-plaster, black and white or brown and cream. Ours and a few others had been given a covering of slates at a period when lath-and plaster was out of fashion. Opposite us was the neo-classical town hall with its *Ratskeller* restaurant and tap-room on the ground floor where I was regularly sent with a tankard to fetch beer for my father's supper. Between our house and the apothecary's ran a narrow lane with very old houses which in former days had lodged court servants, and were now inhabited by artisans and working-class families. Life in the lane was friendly and sociable. Women sat in front of their houses cleaning vegetables for the next meal, knitting or sewing, and exchanging the latest bits of gossip with a neighbour. There were lots of children in the lane, a great source of happiness to an only child who liked company.

Just over the roof of the town hall we could see the trees on the castle ramparts, now the Prince's private gardens. The forecourt of the castle, made into lawns and planted with rows of chestnuts, was bordered by the administrative buildings of the court, the Prince's coach-houses, stables and a splendid stuccoed and mirrored riding-school. The guards at the entrance to the park were changed every few hours, marching from their boxes into the guard-house. We could hear the reveille sounded every morning, and the retreat at night.

The market-place with its church was on the other side of the town hall, and the splashing noise of the water from its decorative fountain, placed right in the middle of the square, was an accustomed and familiar sound day and night. Carts with every conceivable sort of load rolled along the street; huge oxen-drawn ones transported the locally brewed beer, and elegant landaus, rubber-tyred, carried the quality on their outings. Market-days brought waggons full of country produce, and some peasants would walk miles, pulling hand-carts with baskets of butter, eggs, home-made cheese, fruit and vegetables. Live poultry was brought in special cages. Cars were few, and everybody gaped at the doctor's high Daimler steered by a tiller instead of a wheel. Every hour the electric tramcar clanked by, and there were cyclists, the odd daring woman among them. A very pretty woman passsed frequently, wearing a natural-coloured tussore dress and a large straw hat with flowing ribbons. I admired and envied her.

These then were my close surroundings, and who were the people whose life I had come to share?

My father was a man of medium height, bald, with slightly melancholic greenish-brown eyes. He had the sensitive face of an artist or a musician, and his aim had been to follow a career connected with the arts. However, tradition demanded that he should join the family firm to become a draper and linen merchant. He liked fine materials, and had a good knowledge of the art of linen weaving which not so long ago had been a home industry in our part of the world. Past generations of my family had gone as 'agents' to the crofts, and collected for sale the products of the cottage looms. My father was not really interested in business, and he confided in me quite early that he had never wanted to be in commerce. His heart was not in his work, and in many ways his was a wasted life. Before I was ten years old he decided to sell out and live on the income from his investments. Then the shop was let, and so it disappeared from my life. Before that, as a very special favour, I had sometimes been allowed to enter it and look at the fine linens, the printed cottons and lawns that filled its many shelves. All that vanished, and I am sure Father did not regret it. He loved all gentle things, was unworldy, and happiest among his books, at the piano or out in the open. He played the piano well and with ease. His great loves were Haydn and Mozart, and in a gayer mood the romantic operas and waltzes of his youth. He had never liked dancing, but was a regular theatre-goer since boyhood. He had heard all the popular operas over and over again at the court theatre, and could repeat any music he had heard once, by ear, could vary it extempore, and come back to the original theme. His gifts proved valuable when my dancing years came along, and Papa, not always willingly, was promoted to the role of ball pianist. The foxtrots and charlestons of the twenties were a far cry from his repertoire but he played them to perfection, once they had been whistled to him. He even corrected a faulty whistler. Father's other love was literature and its very origin, oral tradition. He had an inexhaustible fund of stories and the patience to tell them again and again. What he lacked perhaps was drive and initiative.

These were supplied in plenty by my mother. She was bright, bustling and very good-looking. Our neighbour, the court-baker used to tell me that when my mother was a bride, he was serving his time with the local regiment. As his platoon passed her on her morning's shopping rounds, the sergeant would give the command: 'Eyes right!', so that all could admire my future mamma. The description of Snow White in the fairytale did fit my mother: white as snow, red as blood, black as ebony. She had a fine fair skin, full red lips, dark eyes, and bluish-black hair. She was the active element in the family, a good housewife and an intelligent cook. She ran the house, planned entertainment and holidays, and chivvied Father when he was in one of his gloomier moods.

For most of my childhood an aunt lived with us, my father's sister. She was a typically Victorian maiden-lady, prim, proper, kind of heart, but difficult for a young child to understand. There were maids, too, and the one I knew longest and loved best was Marie, constant companion of my joys and sorrows.

Through my mother's early anxiety I had as an infant become used to her company and her company only so that I wanted nobody else to attend to me. This did not make me an easy child. When my grandmother on a visit tried to kiss me good-night, I pushed her away, shouting: 'You are an old woman, I want my beautiful mamma!' My 'beautiful mamma' had that night, encouraged by my grandmother who was sick of seeing me, the little horror, spoilt, gone out to dinner with my father. I obstinately kept awake and cried till she returned. I can now see my mother bending over me, dressed in a white foulard gown with tiny black spots, held up, high-waisted, by a royal blue sash.

Only gradually did the fear of being separated from my mother disappear, not actually before I had created a terrible scene at an aunt's wedding. Service and reception over, I refused to be taken back to our hotel by a nanny of some young friends, before the wedding dinner – only for the grown-ups – began. I lay on the red carpet, spread for the bride and groom, in my *broderie anglaise* dress, howling, screaming and kicking my feet in the air. For the sake of peace I was allowed to stay. At eleven o'clock that night I was taken to the hotel in a *droschke* by a gentleman in tails who flattered me by saying I had been the prettiest lady at the party. This I remember clearly and with pleasure, but not what happened after, if anything. Possibly I was too tired to be rebuked and was at once put to bed. The incident, however, was a warning to my mother who gradually forced herself into becoming more detached.

It is certain that memory ignores unpleasantness. My early years have remained in my mind as a succession of happy days, weeks and months. We lived a settled life. There was no sentimentality but much natural affection.

My father had been a bachelor living with two younger brothers and a sister. Whether he had not been interested in women, or whether rumours of the pain of a broken romance were true, I do not know. He was in his forties when my mother, some twenty years younger, came to visit his sister. She arrived late in the afternoon, and was received by the lady of the house alone, who had found it right and proper to send the three men out for a walk so as not to embarrass the visitor by their presence. My mother and aunt-to-be were engaged in polite conversation over the coffee cups when the brothers returned. At the same moment a maid brought in a paraffin lamp, and its light happened to fall on the stranger's face. In a flash, as he said later, one of the brothers realised that his bachelor days were numbered. Here was the woman he could love. After a few days, most daringly, he slipped a poem under the young lady's plate, others followed, and quite soon he proposed. It was love at first sight with my mother too, and he was accepted. The marriage that followed was every bit as happy as the romantic beginning. With quite a big difference in age, and with very different temperaments, they achieved that rare thing, harmony in diversity.

Chapter 2

My year was not divided into neat sections by the calendar, rather was it marked by such red-letter days as 'when the primroses are out in the wood', 'when we gather brambles and rosehips' or 'when we grease the toboggan'. In my memory, summers stand out as hot and sunny while winters were long and very cold. Birthdays were landmarks, not just the parties of friends of my own age, but also the birthdays of older members of the family circle. All were made a great fuss of, and quite distant relations and mere friends exchanged presents.

Naturally Mother's birthday was important. Every year I got a large bunch of snowdrops for her, bought for ten *pfennigs* from a peasant wife in the market. They were small bells, grown in the crofter's garden, of the large wild variety, gathered in the fields by country children. The wild ones smelt best, and sometimes there was an early bright yellow cowslip in the bunch. It was a habit of Mother's to give me a small present on her birthday, an offering of gratitude for 'being born', she explained to me laughingly. A 'birthday table' spread with a fine damask cloth was laid out with presents and flowers the night before, ready to be looked at first thing in the morning. All preparations were made in great secrecy and with much excitement on my part. Poor Mamma was forced to retire early while Father and I set up the table, then pocketed the drawing-room key to make sure all was well. Father was not good at buying presents by himself, so his were often money gifts in pretty coloured envelopes, accompanied by a poem of his own. In a kind of doggerel, he expressed his good wishes, made suggestions on how to spend the money, and, at least in my case, always ended up with a little moral. When I was old enough he impressed on me not to spend everything on either practical things or fripperies, but to let 'the spirit' have its due in the shape of books or tickets for theatres and concerts.

Lunch was a special meal on birthdays, containing invariably one favourite dish of the *Geburtstagskind* – the child born on that day – but best of all was the afternoon party. Cocktails had not yet become popular and parties meant sitting leisurely round a table. Men at these parties were either very young or very old because the middle-aged were busy at work. They might call for their ladies at the end of the afternoon, so something good to eat and drink was kept for them. There was plenty anyway. From four o'clock onwards pots of hot strong coffee appeared on the table laid with fine silver and china. There were bowls of whipped cream, large plates of open sandwiches, and a variety of cakes. The simpler ones would be home-baked, but the richer and more complicated were ordered from the *Hofkonditor*, the pastry cook appointed to the court. He supplied them an hour before the party, packed in tall boxes, rather like hat boxes, and carried by two apprentices, dressed in immaculate white.

Other parties, for the grown-ups only, were given once or twice during the winter. They were usually dinners, and required much preparation. While Mother did the cooking herself, I watched a maid pulling out our heavy dining-room table 'to seat twenty-four'. It was then set, and I was most interested in the place-cards, made by my father. He always laid aside one with my name on it, and this together with some special bits of party food I found on my bedside table next morning. Of the actual party I saw nothing, though I did creep out of bed, and stood looking down the flights of stairs, trying to see the guests arrive. However, this game soon became tedious when the stairs proved much colder than my cosy bedroom where a good anthracite stove burnt day and night. It was a nice stove, iron, with coloured enamel panels, decorated with birds and flowers. Apples could be baked on its hot flat top. Central heating was not installed until some years later. Yet, to sleep in a cold bedroom would have been quite inconceivable.

Fairs were highdays, a number of smaller ones through the year, and the biggest and most interesting one coming round at the end of November, *Andreasmesse* – St. Andrew's Fair. It lasted for three days, and extended over much of the town. Booths were built in all the main streets and for days the sound of hammering was an exciting foretaste of things to come. On the opening day, wrapped up in warm furs, and often tramping through the first snow, my mother and I would go on a visit of inspection. Much Christmas shopping was done at the fair, and we would investigate its possibilities. Also, outlandish things were not stocked in the small shops of our town but the fair brought many to our doorstep. The glove man came from Tyrol, and his booth was decorated with a stuffed chamois. The lace woman from Belgium sold fine motifs for curtains, and these my mother would insert into muslin for new curtains to go up at spring-cleaning time. A stall from Switzerland offered white and pastel-coloured lawns, embroidered and obtainable in dress length. Here I was allowed to make my own choice for next year's summer dress. Dainty china dancers from Meissen were sold on another stall, and in another again gingerbread from Nuremberg, hearts, chocolate-covered or iced, and the little men and women with almonds for buttons on their brown spicy dresses or coats.

A large space was reserved for potters who put out samples of their wares on the ground, unpacking more from straw-filled baskets as sales boomed. Here my mother replenished our supply of kitchen bowls, cups, saucers and large and small plates. To my delight the potter would in the end present me with a few small replicas for my doll's kitchen. About four o'clock it got dark, and the flare lamps were lit in the booths, their strange smell mingling with that of sausages frying on red hot embers; time for the amusement part had come. A square, a little away from the centre of the town, was noisy with people and the music of organs from half a dozen roundabouts. There were booths of performing monkeys, tightrope walkers, 'fat ladies', monsters and haunted houses where awesome 'spectres' would appear at every step. In front of all these sideshows someone stood, shouting, praising the excellence and uniqueness of the performance about to begin. Gipsy women begged to have their hands crossed with silver, and then tell the future. One in particular fascinated me because a large parrot perched on her shoulder, uttering words I could not understand. There were shooting booths with large and small rifles, and hitting a target meant receiving a prize from an enormous glittering display of knick-knacks. I was no good at shooting, but Mother always came away with at least a toy dog – huge and ugly – or one of the then fashionable tea cosies in the shape of a doll with a wide skirt. She liked neither, and handed them on to someone more appreciative.

I enjoyed the roundabouts best, particularly when I rode on one of the fine wooden horses, and many a ten *pfennig* piece went on yet another round. There were peep-shows of disasters and scandals, with a queue of people waiting for the thrill that looking through the tiny holes provided. I remember seeing pictures of the San Francisco earthquake, a few years possibly after it took place. Once or twice I saw a *Moritatensänger*, a man pointing with a long stick to a series of gaudy pictures representing the latest murder, and chanting its story in a monotonous voice. He also told fortunes according to the way a tiny figure moved up and down in a liquid-filled bottle. Wax-figure cabinets, too, catered for the hunger for sensation. One, set up in the market place near us, had a traumatic effect on me which lasted for some years. It was the habit for these wax-work shows to stand a clockwork figure outside to attract attention, and in front of this one stood Prometheus chained to the rock, with the eagle tearing out his liver. I had, of course, no idea what it was all about yet the horror terrified and fascinated me at the same time. I went back to look at it, only to come home shuddering. For a good while I saw Prometheus and the eagle in every dark corner of our rambling house, particularly on the wide staircases at night when I made my way to my bedroom, carrying a candle or a small paraffin lamp.

Winter had its many joys. There was the rare ride in a horse-drawn sledge, and the many outings in a *Stuhlschlitten* – a comfortable seat on runners – pushed by my mother or by Marie when I was small. Tobogganing in the snow-covered woods came later. Most children liked skating on the frozen-over moat. Alas my ankles were not very strong, and I never made much of skating. I was, however, a keen spectator of others who were better at it, and especially of the grown-ups, including my mother, who waltzed to the strings of the regimental band. Now and again there were Gala Nights with coloured lights swinging in the frosty air, and most wonderful to us then, their Serene Highnesses would descend from the castle to walk up and down the rink to the cheers of their loyal subjects. To be commanded on such a night to skate with one of the young princes was the dream-wish of many a local maiden.

From the beginning my father and I were good companions. He was only too glad to leave the shop to an assistant and take me out while Mother busied herself in the house. Quite often the mornings belonged to the two of us. During breakfast – for me a glass of cold milk and a slice of thickly buttered dark rye bread – Father and I would make our plans. If he was to be busy for an hour or two I had time to go up to my room to bathe and dress my collection of dolls. I had many and I liked them. We gave them names according to the countries from which they had been brought as gifts. There was Lisbeth, the Hessian peasant girl, Antoinette from Paris, petite and elegant, Heinerle, a boy from Tyrol, with a big feather on his green felt hat, black-haired Carmen from Spain, Gritje, a pretty Dutch girl, complete with wooden clogs, a sailor-boy from Hamburg, and many others. They lived in a large recess off my bedroom which formed the day nursery. They were eventually joined not by a doll's house but a set of doll's rooms, standing in a row on a low trestle. There was also a small garden complete with swings, a tea pavilion, and a pond made of a mirror on which 'swam' tiny ducks. The doll's household was a miniature double of our own, with small sets of glasses, china and cutlery, and even a linen chest full of household linen, sewn by my mother, and embroidered with a tiny R. I laid my dolls' table just like our own. The dolls' kitchen was equipped with a spirit stove, and there, supervised by my mamma, I cooked my first meal of pancakes and apple sauce. The minute frying pan made delicious pancakes, about one inch and a half in diameter, to be served to the dolls and to my friends at a low white table in the nursery. The family of dolls was watched over by a small black poodle, knitted by an aunt when I was a baby. It remained one of my favourite toys, rivalled perhaps only by Peter, the jumping-jack whose cheerful moustachioed face I loved.

Some days I filled in the early hours with visits to neighbours. I always called first on Karl, the court baker, a stoutish middle-aged man with a round jolly face. Many things contributed to making him my favourite. He was cheerful and patient with me, and last but not least, he owned a horse. I was fond of horses, and never had any fear of them. It was my greatest wish to ride one. There was not the slightest chance of my owning a pony or even having riding lessons. However, Karl took his freshly baked morning rolls on a small cart to nearby villages. The cart was drawn by a beautiful chestnut horse, and when he came back from his rounds, just about the time I had finished my breakfast, he took the empty baskets into his shop, and then led the horse and cart through the lane by the side of our house to the stable. I watched him eagerly from a window. One morning he waved me to come out and then asked me whether I would care to ride the horse to the stable. Would I not? To me it was a sheer miracle to be allowed to ride a real horse. Karl lifted me on to the huge beast, and from that moment I never missed my morning ride whatever the weather. It was from Karl that I first learned that horses need special shoes in snow, and that one has to take care not to be hard on their mouth. He told me to hold on to the mane in case I felt myself slipping, but I soon forgot about that, and balanced proud and confident as any circus rider.

My love for the baker's horse forged a bond between Karl and myself, and he began taking me straight from the stable into his bakehouse. It was warm, spotlessly clean, and full of lovely smells. I watched the baker and his boys in their white coats and high chef's hats taking out loaf after loaf on long-handled wooden shovels from a roaring big oven. The loaves varied in shape and colour, from the fine white 'french' bread to the almost black Westphalian rye. Though I was never very fond of cake, Karl knew my weakness for his very special *Zwieback* – the german for rusk, and meaning twice baked – and he allowed me to taste it now and then, before and after the second baking which is actually more of a toasting. The rusks started as a very light sponge, pure eggs, butter and sugar, and just a suggestion of flour. Flour with him was flour, nothing taken away and nothing added, and eggs, butter and cream he brought fresh from the farm on his morning runs. Sometimes I went with Karl on his cart to the mill to fetch flour. There were three mills in the town then, the upper and lower one,and the mill in the centre, called *Obere*, *Untere*, and *Mittel Mühlr*. Hens scratched for stray grains of corn in the grounds around the mill, and ducks swam on the ponds. I fed them with bits of stale bread while Karl collected his sacks. The mills were resounding with the noise of huge stone grinders, and somewhere the miller appeared from clouds of flour dust. The air was full of the scent of ripe corn.

My next favourite on the morning visits was a man in a workshop in the lane. His job was mending china and antiques. He was a tall man with a sallow complexion who spoke in a manner different from the people round about, and his slightly strange ways intrigued me as much as his work. I could watch him making a tiny rose of some material or other, colour it, and fit it on to a Dresden candlestick where one small flower had been knocked off. Franz also took great care in putting my broken toys together again, and once made me a whole new head for a doll that had come to grief.

In the side-streets near us there were many old-fashioned shops in basements where one had to go down a few steps to reach the counter. A bell tinkled at the door, and such rare things as sour cream, poured out freshly, were sold. Also, butter and cheese, fresh from the farm, and rolled in leaves to keep them cool. In quite a few places drams were dispensed to tired workmen and carters who had got cold on their high seats. Gin, Kümmel or rum were measured out into small glasses, then drunk in one quick gulp. A strange old watchmaker collected rarities which he showed in his shop window. He had a clock which went for a hundred days without winding, and piles of stones and crystals, collected on walks. After a court hunt rows of deer could be seen hung up at a venison dealer's who also kept carp in big basins, to be killed only shortly before being cooked. Carp was very popular and made a delicious meal, either steamed with a savoury sauce, fried or stuffed.

The most frequent calls I had to make for my mother were to the grocer's only a few houses away. The things I had to get were mostly pretty ordinary: pepper, salt, flour and sugar. Sugar was special only when I had to carry home a whole *Zuckerhut*. This was a whole loaf of sugar, wrapped in dark-blue paper, and used for making jam or preserving fruit. The apothecary's next door was by far the most interesting. The apothecary himself was a quiet, scholarly man whom I regarded with some awe. His young assistants were less frightening. With them I could chat freely and receive answers to my questions. They were prepared to show me wonderful glass bottles of all shapes and sizes, also jars and pots bearing strange names which the young men tried to make me pronounce. If I still knew the names when next I called, I was rewarded with a stick of liquorice. I learned some herb lore from them too, as they showed me flowers and leaves hung up to dry, eventually to be used for brewing tisanes. I already knew camomile, peppermint and lime flower, my mother's regular cure-alls.

I also became friendly with the Prince's blue-liveried grooms in the stables almost opposite our house. I could go in and see the beautiful horses being prepared for a ride or carriage drive. I sat on the straw in a corner for hours watching what went on. Nobody bothered about me.

The counts and ruling princes had been interested in horses for centuries, and a stud was established not far from their capital. Tradition had it that the horses' distant ancestors were Roman ones captured in battle. Arab stallions were introduced later, and mares were not fed by hand, summer or winter, but found their food in the woods, scratching for heather even under the snow. This made for the survival of the fittest, and produced a sturdy good-looking horse which, eventually crossed with English breeds, was in great demand.

Extensive beechwoods were within easy reach, and with Father I tramped their broad rides and soft narrow paths. They were my first schoolroom where I learnt the names of trees, birds, and flowers, their habitat and their habits. The woods held many treasures: dog violets and anemones in the spring, brambles and rosehips in the autumn, and branches of fir for Christmas. Now and again my mother would send us to the *Lustgarten*, a former pleasance, turned into kitchen gardens which sold produce to the public. An old court gardener took us round the neat, box-trimmed vegetable beds and allowed us to choose whatever cauliflower, lettuce or tender green peas or beans we fancied. He grew flowers, too, and on a fine summer morning the broad borders were ablaze with colour. Sometimes, and as a very special enterprise, Father would decide to take the local train for a short journey. We would get out near a *Krug*, a country inn where ploughmen and foresters in their green uniforms had a drink, and the farmers, too, who stopped on their way to market. We sat down at a cleanly scrubbed table, placed in front of a bench running along the length of a wall. There we ate the buttered bread Mother had prepared, perhaps with a hard-boiled egg and a bunch of radishes. Father would order a *Helles* – a glass of Lager beer – and I would get a beaker of milk fresh from the cow, as most innkeepers were farmers also. It was the general habit for people to bring their own food, and only order drink though food – hot and cold – was served if required. Afterwards Father and I would walk back some five or six miles thoroughly contented with our adventure.

On these outings we met many people who knew my father, woodmen, shepherds and crofters. For a generation or two my father's firm had supplied the whole trousseau for many a country bride. Trousseaus were very considerable then, and I remember elderly men telling my father how well the linens supplied by the firm were doing. Sheets, towels and tablecloths then had to last for life. In my grandfather's day the girls would do their own spinning and weaving, but would ask his firm to make up the household linen, bedding, pillows and quilts, often filled with feathers from the home farmyards. All these activities made for a close relationship with the firm and its owners, and through his great integrity Father was a well-loved figure.

In his young days he and his brothers were frequently invited to farm weddings. These were tremendous affairs, lasting for days on end, with music and dancing, and much eating and drinking. He once told me of a wedding where there had been a competition among the young men as to who could eat the most hard-boiled eggs. Father also told me how once the Devil had lured the musicians from a wedding to feast at his infernal abode where they were richly rewarded for their playing. In the morning, however, they found themselves lying under the gallows, with their gold turned into cow dung. Later I found the very same story in the manuscripts of the Brothers Grimm. Father was a wonderful storyteller, and I was very interested in the tales he told about places we visited. He knew many, told to him by his father, and he was also a keen reader of historical accounts and old chronicles of the district. Also, he could make up a story on the spur of the moment.

For many years I believed firmly in Father Christmas and also in the German tradition of the *Osterhase*, the hare that brings the eggs for Easter. We knew a little hut in the woods, possibly a worker's toolshed, where the Easter Hare lived. In the spring we passed the hut very quietly in order not to disturb the Hare while he was busy colouring eggs, at least Father said so. 'Any special eggs you would like?' he then used to ask. 'We might pop a line under the door.' And seated on the moss outside we, that is Father, would write a little note of instructions to the Easter Hare. Eggs 'with faces' I liked best, and when we all went to the woods at Easter to search for eggs, supposedly hidden there by the Hare, I found beautiful eggs with laughing faces, with crying ones, with baby faces, and some quite grotesque ones, with the faces of pirates and bandits, their fierce eyes glaring. Years after I found out that my good papa had spent hours drawing faces in black ink on the eggs my mother had dyed previously. Onion skin dyed the eggs a bright orange.

Easter was the time for our first picnic. The party might include four or five children, neighbours and friends. Somehow one or two grown-ups managed to disappear for a few minutes to hide the coloured eggs they had brought with them, in the moss around trees or in tiny nests made up quickly from grass and fallen leaves. When all the eggs were disposed of round the picnicking place, Father would clap his hands and chant:

'Der Has' hat gelegt ins grüne Gras
Kommt all herbei und holt euch was'

indicating that the Hare had hidden eggs in the green grass, and that the search should begin. It was fun hunting for the eggs, and shouts of joy accompanied every find. Eventually the company settled to a meal of hard-boiled eggs, bread and butter. Some eggs were kept for eating on the following days. We hardly ever had chocolate eggs, but when I was a little older I was given some cardboard eggs, covered with colour-printed paper, and filled with a handkerchief, a pair of gloves or, height of delights, a small bottle of violet-scented cologne.

My taste for the savoury rather than the sweet had its embarrassing moments when on visits to friends I refused creamcakes and sweetmeats, yet was too shy to ask for bread and butter. Eventually my mamma wrote an apologetic little note to my prospective hostesses, explaining. Then, to my joy, bread and butter was put down for me. One day I was ill with a painful inflammation of the ear. I could not sleep, so there were tears and great discomfort. A good father tried to soothe my troubles and forgetting for a moment, promised me chocolate in the morning if I would try and go to sleep. I was told later that even in my distress I remembered, and a faint little voice said 'Not chocolate, *Leberwurst*, please'. Liver sausage was my height of gastronomic pleasures. I liked the story of *Red Ridinghood* which I had told to me over and over again, but when it came to the bit where the girl takes cake and wine to her sick grandmother, I made it clear that liver sausage and wine would be much better, and liver sausage and wine it was ever after.

Fairytales were very real to me. I should have found it strange had anybody questioned the existence of fairies. The wind, the rain, the sun, the moon, all were personified to me, and I located the happenings of fairytales in my daily surroundings. In a nearby forest once stood Sleeping Beauty's castle. Had not Father shown me the briar bushes, the very last to remain of the great rose hedge that surrounded the castle? A high hill, rather forbiddingly covered with rugged trees and heather, was one of the seven hills which separated me from Snow White and the Seven Dwarfs. How often did I look up that hill hoping that I might catch sight of one of the "little men" on my way home from gathering berries. But then, their berry-gathering was done at night, I was told.

Ours was certainly done in the daytime with Marie on many a summer's afternoon. To pick bilberries we each took an old cup, and when it was full, emptied it into a basket. Marie had a special method of getting berries quickly by 'combing' the bushes. For this she kept a specially wide comb which she had brought from the farm where she was born. I just used my fingers, and by the time I had finished they were black because over-ripe berries did get squashed, and many disappeared into my equally black mouth anyhow. We ate our sandwiches with a bottle of home-made raspberry juice before setting out on the hour's walk back. If I had been a good picker and not too impatient, Marie might tell me one of her stories on the way. These were not all gentle. Many a tale contained stern warnings, and one in particular said that 'a sinner's hand will grow out of the grave to proclaim his sin', a pretty frightening picture for a little girl who took it all in open-mouthed, and even asked for more.

'Sin' was mentioned quite often and in connection with quite small matters. Waste above all was 'sin'. This meant never asking for more than one could eat up, and not ever leaving bits and pieces on the plate. I learned to make spills from odd pieces of paper which would have been wasted otherwise, for Father to light his pipe – no waste of matches. This teaching was all linked with a healthy respect for money and the need to save whenever possible.

This deep-seated conviction was sadly demolished when years later inflation struck Germany, and all savings were lost.

Modernity in the shape of the first cinema, called *Kino*, came to our town when I was about five years old. It was a very primitive affair, installed in the back premises of one of our neighbours, but it was mystery and enchantment to a child who knew only the coloured slides of the *Lanterna Magica*, the magic lantern which projected still pictures on to a white surface – mostly a stretched tablecloth – in a dark room. The *Kino* was mystery because there were only vague allusions to it in the conversation of adults. Enchantment it became soon because a way was found to gain admittance and find out what it was all about. An elderly woman was the one and only usher in charge of conducting the audience to their seats. Seeing crowds of children look longingly into the darkness when the door of the miraculous place opened for a second, her heart softened. Putting her finger to her lips to indicate absolute quietness and good behaviour she pushed four or five of us inside. There we sat, as quiet and good as church mice, looking at the flickering picture on the screen. It was accompanied by lilting music from a piano which added to the enchantment. The first film I ever saw, was *Sledge Bells* or *A Mysterious Murder*, showing the hunt for the murderer through deep snow. I do not remember the story, and, of course, I would not see the whole of it as we were thrown out when the next lot came. Anyhow, we indulged in this very secret entertainment for a while.

The other innovation was the advent of an Italian ice-cream maker, one Luigi da Viga. He was interesting to us, and though I did not much care for sweet stuff, this new ice-cream in all the colours of the rainbow did hold attractions. For reasons best known to themselves, our elders and betters were not keen on us eating the ice-cream, and we were told that poor Luigi made it with his feet. His 'factory' was in a basement, and we spent hours lying flat on our tummies looking through the grating over the basement windows to find out how he actually did make it. Alas, we never knew the truth, and for us ice-cream remained a treat, made by mothers on rare occasions, in huge complicated wooden tubs, with the help of natural ice and special salt.

PART II

Growing Up

Chapter 3

People assure me that they themselves or their children longed to go to school, and even more, longed to learn to read, and to be with other children. I did not. What I learned daily from my father seemed quite enough. Everything in nature became more and more familiar to me, and in poor weather we sat in Father's study looking at pictures in his many books while he told me all about them. One of them showed how a printing machine works, and another how James Watt watched his mother's kettle boiling, and became aware of the power of steam.

There was much to explore with Father.

To be one in a class with a crowd of little girls did not interest me either. Though I was an only child, I was never lonely. I could always find something to do, and if I wanted company there were plenty of children around to play with. The fairly strict separation of 'the classes' had not prevented my parents from allowing me to choose my own playmates, and my favourites were the boys and girls in the lane behind our house. The sons and daughters of my parents' friends were a little too well-behaved for me. In the lane there were large families, and the boys often let me share their outdoor games. At the slightest sound of a whistle – they whistled by putting the second and third finger to their mouth – I would be out for a game of 'cops and robbers', or what the boys called 'cutting out land'. This was a strange game, not without much danger. I am told that I was rescued from it at a tender age, just before a boy's pocket knife landed in my back. On a piece of unpaved ground a boy would mark out a large square with his heels. Then on each side of this, and facing it, a child would lie down flat on his tummy. From this position he or she would throw a pocket knife into the square, and up to the point where it landed the ground would be his or hers. Frontiers changed rapidly while tension grew, and he who after so many rounds, I have forgotten just how many, had the biggest piece, was declared 'King'.

We also played endless games with marbles, and there was excitement as big, beautiful, coloured glass ones changed hands. For hopping games the boys marked the pavement with chalk, and when the wind was right we ran to an open field to fly kites. Kites, looking like fabulous animals, could be bought for a few pennies. They were made in the Far East, I imagine, and rose better than all others. They had long and complicated tails. Once I had a real 'dragon', and strangely enough *Drachen* is the German name for a kite. I did not join in the boys shooting with their *Flitzebogen* – home-made bows – and arrows, but sat with them in the lane colouring cheap little wooden spinning tops which we then whipped along the streets. I had insisted on learning to roller-skate in spite of my weak ankles but I gave it up after a nasty fall.

Our street was a happy playground, with little traffic to disturb us.

In my last pre-school summer I was seized by a sudden passion for learning to swim. My mother was a keen swimmer, and went regularly to the local swimming bath, a specially laid out section of the river. Men and women were strictly separated by high screens of sail-cloth. In the women's section stood a number of huts, each about the size of a large sitting-room, for those who wanted to do their bathing in private. The huts could be hired by the hour, and my mother took one about twice a week all through the summer. Since I had become the proud owner of a bathing-suit, buttoned on the shoulders, with little frills around the ankles, I went with her. I could sit on the steps leading into the water, and even swing on a bar suspended above. But, what I wanted was to be able to swim like Mother. Her tuition inside the hut was not very successful, and it was decided that I should have proper lessons from a retired sergeant. Reporting to him at the open basin, I was put into a wide leather belt fixed to a strong wooden pole which the sergeant held over the water. At his command I was to make the first strokes. But unknown to me, he had a special method of hardening his pupils. Once they were suspended over the water, he suddenly ducked them. With me the procedure had quite the opposite effect. I was terrified and came up screaming. The sergeant pulled me out of the water. There was much shouting as he unwillingly took off the contraption. Still shaking with fright I went home with my mother, and when my hysterics had settled, I made up my mind that I would learn to swim but definitely without the sergeant.

One of my friends in the lane had learnt on 'tins', and to his house I went to tell my tale. He could now swim without aids, and generously offered me the use of his 'tins'. These were two large containers in which our grocer had kept Maggi's soup cubes. 'Maggi' was written across them in large red letters on a yellow ground. The lids had been soldered on to the tins, and they were joined by a wide piece of linen for a belt. As soon as I lay down on this belt in the water I floated happily and without fear. I went to the swimming bath day after day, carefully avoiding the hours when the sergeant was on duty. And I succeeded: in a month's time I could swim. My poor mother never got her money back for the twelve swimming lessons she had paid for in advance.

The thought of school became more and more daunting in the peaceful spring of 1912. In Germany the school year began in April, and no child under six years of age was admitted. My birthday being in October, I was six and a half years old by then. Everybody impressed on me how lovely it would be to go to school soon, and I was bought a fine light-brown leather satchel. I had liked nice things from a very early age but the new satchel with the prospect of school failed to cheer me.

About this time news came that I was to be bridesmaid to a cousin sixteen years my senior. My first day at school was to coincide with the wedding. Also, my father told me that on that very day there would be an eclipse of the sun. The sky would get dark in the middle of the day, and that was the moment the moon would pass across the sun. With some luck, it could all be watched through a tiny piece of blackened glass. This and the wedding were interesting events, and somewhat took the sting out of the dreaded 'going to school'.

A dress was ordered for the wedding, shoes, stockings and underwear. My own choice was taken into acccount, and I remember that I was allowed to have pale-blue silk ribbon threaded through the Swiss embroidered lawn of my panties and petticoat – something I had longed for. To heighten the excitement a young cousin and I were to strew flowers from small baskets in front of the newly married couple on their return to the carriage. This appealed to me, and for weeks we rehearsed 'strewing flowers' with tiny bits of paper. We were told to walk slowly and evenly to give the bridal couple the chance of advancing gracefully behind us. Father played Mendelssohn's Wedding March on the piano to give us the right rhythm. It was all very grand.

At long last the day of the great events arrived – the 12th of April – and Mother took me to school that morning. There were some thirty other mothers with their daughters, and all these little girls had one thing in common. They were *Höhere Töchter*, daughters of the bourgeoisie. The equivalent of the later *Lyzeum* was then the very class-conscious *Höhere Töchterschule*, a fee-paying municipal High School for girls. It provided a ten years' course, with the main stress on the arts and modern languages. Mathematics and science took second place though their importance increased during my time at school.

Boys and girls of 'the lower classes' went to the *Bürgerschule,* and one of the great distinctions was that while the High School children began writing in copy books with a pencil, 'they' used a slate and a slate pencil with a small sponge to wipe the slate clean. This sponge was fixed to the slate by a piece of string, and kept hanging out of the satchel, which boys and girls carried on their backs. Not to have a sponge hang from the satchel was a definite status symbol.

On that first morning at school we all had big white, pink, or blue silk bows on top of our heads, and hair falling loose to the shoulders. Soon it would be tamed into schoolgirl plaits.

Everybody appeared happy, and with great glee the children received from their future teacher a huge coloured paper bag full of sweets. This was a custom observed on the first schoolday. Parents bought the big, pointed bags and took them to the school a day or two earlier. Then they were presented to the children, to curry favour, I suppose. I was not amused, and stubbornly refused to be photographed with the thing. Next day I distributed the sweets among my boy friends in the lane. The pointed bag – upside down – served as a sorcerer's hat in our games.

In spite of my unwillingness to accept school I did like our teacher, a friendly woman with a big bun of chestnut-brown hair. She wore lace blouses with tight fish bone supported collars, and had a soft gentle voice. In our first lesson we copied the letter i from the blackboard, and I carried home my copybook with a few lines of the letter running up and down the page, yet just recognisable. The copy book was soon forgotten when Mother helped to dress me for the wedding. I do not remember much about it, except that I had hidden a little piece of blackened glass in my flower basket. The sky was darkening when the bride and bridegroom left after the wedding service, and I nearly stopped the procession when I groped for my piece of glass, forgetting all about the pace I was to keep. Fortunately we had almost reached the carriage, and I soon scampered away and, assisted by my understanding father, actually saw the eclipse.

School went on drearily since I grudged the time away from Father's company and the games in the lane. I endlessly copied letters from the blackboard, yet when it came to putting these letters together to form a word, my performance was hopeless. M-a-m-m-a was all right, but that these queer symbols represented the familiar word 'Mamma', was a fact I could or would not grasp. My mother, who had taken over the supervision of my homework, became exasperated, and, as I was told later, after she had had a talk with my equally exasperated teacher, this teacher talked to me seriously one day:

'I hear' she said, 'you like stories. Now I'm sure you would like to be able to read them.' I can still hear my resounding: 'No', and her: 'But why?' 'Because my father knows them all, and can tell them to me.'

There was silence after that.

It took the better part of six months to overcome my resistance to formal learning. Then, suddenly, I came out of my private world, and equally suddenly I could read. I remember distinctly the feeling of achievement mixed with disappointment, because Father's stories could never be quite the same again. This, of course, is an adult recollection, but I do remember that at the time I was not completely happy about being able to read. I still preferred my father's study to the classroom. There I could look at so many books without being forced to read them. Father liked books not for their contents alone. He liked them as objects. He liked to touch fine binding, and even the smell of leather of a well-bound volume gave him pleasure. He showed me the tooling on spines, and many hand-coloured plates of birds and flowers, often the very same we had seen on our walks. Thus he had made me like and respect books when reading them was still a little irksome.

About that time Father taught me how to make a herbarium. Plants and leaves, brought home from our walks, were carefully pressed between blotting paper, with first one or two and then a pile of books on them. When the specimens were dry we mounted them on large sheets which went into a loose-leaf album. We then wrote the plants' names underneath, together with the place where we had found them. I also began collecting picture postcards, and putting them into albums. At school we swapped scraps and *Lesezeichen*, bookmarks, embroidered or silk-painted, and for a time a craze for transfers made me cover the doors of my wardrobe, chests and backs of chairs with all kinds of flower arrangements, and scenes of angelic pink-faced children, trundling hoops. The collecting of

Reklamemarken became a fashion. These were issued by all kinds of industrial firms, either singly or in series, forerunners perhaps of cigarette cards. They were printed, some very beautifully, on thin gummed paper, to be pasted into albums. There were historical series, birds, flowers, flags, heraldic designs, nonsense verses and many others.

With all these new activities, with at least four hours lesssons at school, including Saturdays, and homework during the afternoons, I had now much less time for outings with Father. A great many hours went into learning to spell and repeating the multiplication table.

Yet there were compensations.

Though I remained faithful to my companions in the lane, I made friends with girls in my class, and was invited to their homes. One or two were farmers' daughters, and to spend a day with them in the country was a new and exciting experience. The lath-and-plaster farm houses were spacious and comfortable. People and animals lived under one roof. Through a large door, wide enough to allow for the passage of carts, horses and cows, one entered a square hall with the hayloft above. Animals lived on one side of the hall, and the family on the other. On these country visits I came to know many dishes which were not cooked at home. One of my favourites was *Pickert*, savoury potato pancakes, fried in oil. In the poorer parts of the country where potatoes did not grow, pancakes were made of buckwheat, and very good they were. I liked home-made farm cheese, flavoured with herbs or caraway seeds, plenty of milk, cream and fruit in season. Berries, picked fresh from the bushes, tasted quite different. And it was a great treat to be taken home on a farm cart drawn by one or two beautiful horses, when I was allowed to sit next to the coachman.

The mothers of school friends in the town provided us with more sophisticated pleasures. We went to a *Konditorei*, a pastry shop where people took cakes and coffee on the premises in a small room with plush-upholstered chairs and marble-topped tables. In spite of my preference for the savoury, I enjoyed going to the counter to choose one of the luscious confections displayed. This was then brought to the table with something to drink, hot chocolate for the children, while the mothers indulged in mocha and whipped cream. In the summer we sometimes went to a hotel in the main street of our little town where tables and chairs were set out on the pavement, sheltered by high-trained ivy in green-painted boxes. Mothers watched the passers-by, but we just gobbled and giggled.

Before I went to school I had once been taken to the theatre to see a fairytale play, *Frau Holle*. The story tells of the two daughters of a poor widow, one pretty and industrious, the other ugly and idle. They were rewarded and punished respectively by *Mother Holle*, the Earth Mother of German folklore. I remember how the good girl came out of a well, covered with gold, while the bad one was covered with black pitch. I also remember the whole audience rising when the young Princess and her governess entered the Prince's box.

The theatre itself was elegant. It was the old court theatre which had existed in one form or another since the eighteenth century. To begin with, travelling players had performed in the town hall or at court where ladies and gentlemen, princes and princesses had taken part in the acting. A very simply equipped *Komödienhaus* was built at the end of the eighteenth century, and even this quite primitive theatre had been held in high respect. Art-loving princes who encouraged and financed play-acting and music created a theatre tradition well beyond that of a small town. Leading actors thought it an honour to perform as guests at the court theatre. Through his own father and other older theatre-loving members of the family, my father had a store of tales about the theatre's early days. At one time all box-office takings went to the local poor. The theatre-going public was served with tea, coffee, cake and a variety of wines, to which the actors and musicians were also treated. Family legend has it that my grandfather attended concerts conducted by Brahms during his short stay at the court, and the composer Lortzing belonging to the theatre troupe, was still a living memory. His tuneful romantic operas remained favourites in the repertoire.

Soon after my first visit the court theatre burnt to the ground during a cold February night, and was not rebuilt for many years.

Visits to the theatre created in me a taste for dressing up and for acting. The mother of one of my friends had a liking for *Tableaux Vivants*, and with improvised props she dressed us and taught us to stand in certain positions to represent one of the fashionable 'conversation pieces' or a scene from a fairytale. I once 'played' the three drops of blood in the tale of *The Goose Girl*. It was a speaking part, and over and over I had to say the solemn words: 'If this your mother knew, her heart would break in two.' My costume consisted of a white apron on which had been sewn three large red patches in the shape of drops.

There were also fancy-dress parties, particularly at Carnival time. I disliked frilly things, and 'boys' suited me best. So I presented a succession of them: the kitchen boy from *Sleeping Beauty*, with a long wooden spoon in my belt as the mark of my trade, fairytale *Hänsel*, from *Hänsel and Gretel*, a stable boy, and the little 'blackamaoor' the well known trademark of a German chocolate firm.

School holidays had become important events. Many were spent at my uncle's house in Marburg. I had grown very fond of this town built on hills above the valley of the river Lahn, with many steep streets, and flights of steps, ideal for playing hide and seek with my young cousins and their friends. Here I saw for the first time a performing bear. Standing on its hind legs it danced to the rhythm of a tambourine played by the bear-leader. I was fascinated and ran up quite close to the bear which suddenly hit out at me with its paw. Only through the quick-witted bear-leader pushing me over while pulling his bear away, was I saved from trouble. I never again went close to a dancing bear though I did see many more in years to come. Another exciting thing in Marburg was seeing the maids in my uncle's household and all country people coming into town wearing *Tracht*, the special costume of the region. This was colourful, the women wearing an enormously wide pleated skirt, made buoyant by a number of petticoats, one on top of another. The girls wore their hair piled high, with a tiny red cap to crown it. Some say that this very cap gave the Brothers Grimm the title of their tale *Little Red*

Ridinghood, when they were collecting tales in that region of Hesse. The tale itself is, however, much older, and Perrault's *Chaperon Rouge* was known more than a hundred years before the Grimms.

Students, too, lent colour to Marburg's street life with their head-gear of many shapes and colours. Colours and shapes might indicate one of the many student associations they belonged to. Then there was the green-uniformed local regiment, the *Jäger*, marching through the town with their band playing. At their head rode an officer in a splendid elaborate uniform, a big plume on his high shako.

Other holidays were spent at Hanover, the first 'big' city I ever saw. The shops there were marvellous, particularly the stores where things never dreamt of in our little town could be seen. In Hanover, too, I admired military splendour when the *Uhlans* dashed through the town on horseback, their yellow-and-blue coloured Guelph pennants streaming from their high-held lances. There were parades in the handsome royal domain of Herrenhausen.

It was during my early years at school that I was made aware of being Jewish. Sure enough, I had been taken to services at the synagogue, but it had not meant much to me. 'Organised religion' never appealed to me. My father's family were practising Jews, though rumour had it that two pretty girls eloped in the early nineteenth century with Napoleonic officers, and that somewhere in France a Catholic/Jewish strain of the family must be living. Officially, however, this connection was never discussed. My mother's family held liberal religious views, and there were mixed marriages in past generations and in the present one. From a very early age both parents had impressed on me that colour, creed, race or religious beliefs were immaterial against the background of a general humanity. Being born into a Jewish family did not make me feel 'different' in any way.

At school I was told that I was to take part in special religious instruction arranged for Jewish children, and was not expected to attend the general Morning Assembly. Neither arrangement pleased me, and I continued to go to Morning Assembly to sing the same hymns as all my friends. I came to love the Lord's Prayer, and often repeated it to myself, especially at night in the dark when the thought of that chained Prometheus still came over me. I had a vague feeling that the 'good God', a friendly father figure, should belong to everyone in the same way.

Disillusionment was to come.

Chapter 4

As the years went by the reluctant reader had become a ferocious one. No books were barred, and the shelves of my father's study were a treasure house to which I escaped whenever possible. I still had a great love for tales and legends, and now read many of the stories I had at one time been told by Father. German tales were followed by those of other countries when the tales of classical Antiquity became my great favourites.

I liked historical subjects, and began reading plays by Schiller, Goethe and Lessing. I made the acquaintance of Shakespeare in Schlegel and Tieck's translation, and enjoyed all this rather heavy meat along with my mother's favourite novelists, Wilhelm Raabe, Theodor Storm and Selma Lagerlöf. Her story of Niels Holgersen's magic journey became my bedside reading for many months. Amidst all else I came back again and again to the emotionally stirring tales of Hans Christian Andersen, and, of course, to the Grimms' Household Tales which never frightened me. For a little while I was addicted to *Mädchenbücher*, stories about girls in their teens with whom I secretly identified, sharing their romantic lives which culminated usually in an engagement to some dashing lieutenant or other desirable male.

I began to be interested in boys merely from a 'decorative' point of view. I had started to take piano lessons, and it was distinctly 'decorative' to have a High School boy lingering in the street below my teacher's house, ready to see me home at the end of the lesson and carry my music case. My father took a poor view of this practice, and my more indulgent mother advised me to come home by the side-streets where Father would not watch for us. This was a pity as in these side-streets not so many people would observe my escort, yet it was expedient, and 'the boys' would be dismissed at a suitable distance from our house. Every Sunday morning the regimental band played for an hour in the castle gardens. There we went, three or four schoolgirls, arms linked, waiting for the thrilling moment when from a distance some High School boys would raise their coloured caps to us. Part of our own street was a place for strolling in the early hours of the evening. Beside the many *Pensionsmädel* – girls in the fashionable Finishing Schools – taken in 'crocodiles' by their teachers, and receiving salutes from their young men, we were very small fry. All the same, hours for the *Bummel* were kept strictly in all weathers, and homework hurried through to be ready in good time.

I had not inherited Father's musical gifts, and my piano playing never got very far. However, my teacher was a civilised woman who helped me to an understanding of music, and, what is even more, I absorbed what could be broadly called 'culture' in the special atmosphere of her home. With her old mother she lived on the upper floor of a fine old house, and after I had run up the flight of stairs with their wrought iron railings, I was in a world apart. My teacher wore long flowing gowns in bright colours made to her own design, coral or amber beads and large brooches, sometimes with a few flowers pinned to her dress. The flat was full of beautiful old furniture, pictures and objets d'art. She had a special love for *Biedermeier*, that early nineteenth-century German style which produced furniture of simple pleasing lines, made mostly from orchard woods. If there was an interval between pupils arriving, I would be invited to stay for a cup of hot chocolate and to what amounted to another lesson in art, design or even social history of her favourite period. Through my teacher I became myself enthusiastic about anything called *Biedermeier*. During some repairs in our house when paraffin lamps and gas light were replaced by electricity, Mother decided that one of the guest rooms should now be turned into a sitting-room/study for me. To equip my room we went up to the attics where a lot of furniture of former generations was stored, and there we unearthed some dusty old pieces which to my delight were pure *Biedermeier.* A restorer, a dedicated craftsman, removed layers of grime and paint, and I became the proud owner of fine tables, chairs, a china cabinet, and a desk. He made a bookcase in cherry wood to match the rest.

During the summer months the *Sommertheater* in the hall of an inn on the outskirts of the town provided entertainment. It often employed eminent actors who were 'resting' and was known for its high standard of performance. My parents had a subscription for this theatre for one night a week, and I frequently accompanied them to the door. I was never taken into the theatre as my bedtime, summer and winter, was eight o'clock, except on very special occasions. True, I was allowed to read in bed, and was even given a bedside lamp after my mother discovered that I was secretly keeping a torch under the mattress. Eventually the summer theatre became available to me in the same way as the cinema had a few years earlier. An elderly usher took pity on the children who accompanied their parents to the door and were then turned back, and she waved us in the moment the lights were dimmed, and the curtain rose. She allowed us to stand at the back for one act only, after which we had to tiptoe out, and get home to our beds as quickly as our feet would carry us in order to avoid bringing trouble to our kind protectress. I saw the first act of many a play and operetta long before I came to know the whole, a fact my parents were blissfully unaware of. But these glimpses of the magic world of the stage, even if irregular, made me an ardent addict. In the quietness of my bedroom I tried to make up the rest of the play, and was convinced firmly that some day I would be an actress or perhaps a dancer. Often my private evening finished with improvised dances in front of the bedroom mirror. I had no singing voice but I managed to hum a tune I had heard several times, and thus I became intoxicated with imaginary glamour.

School went smoothly, and life seemed good in the early summer of 1914. Then, one day in late June my aunt came running into the sitting-room to announce that she had read in the paper about the assassination of the Austrian archduke Franz Ferdinand. She was excited and kept shouting: 'This means war, this means war!' I had no idea what it was all about, nor did I know why the grown-ups looked concerned, and in the weeks to come kept talking about things I did not understand. The word 'ultimatum' turned up in their conversation again and again. War was to become a reality to me quite soon.

On the 1st August my father took me to the barracks to see the mobilisation orders for army and navy, signed by the *Kaiser*, posted on large white sheets pasted on the red brick walls.

In the barrack yards high-spirited volounteers were gathering, flowers in their buttonholes, clamouring to be put into uniform. There was a kind of mad gaiety about, as if they were preparing for a celebration or a great enjoyable adventure, with shouts of: 'The war will be over by Christmas.' There was much hurrahing and singing. This was the moment for my father to make clear to me that war was evil and senseless. It was barbarous to shoot and kill people, and he hoped I would always remember this day as a tragic one whatever the outcome of the war might be. For the first time in my life I saw tears in his eyes, and I never forgot. On our way home we heard planes overhead, *Rumplertauben* bound for the front, we were told. These monoplanes were called 'Rumpler's pigeons' after their inventor, Rumpler of Vienna.

At school the atmosphere became hectic and very pro-war. Girls began wearing black-white-and-red ribbons in their hair, brooches with patriotic slogans on their dresses and small replicas of the Iron Cross became popular pendants.

The quick march of the German armies through Belgium led to jubilation and days off at school to celebrate victories. I enjoyed the holidays as much as anybody, but I was never quite easy in my mind and could not join in the general excitement. My father kept looking sad and very worried, and I have a vague memory of how he spoke to me in sorrow about the burning of the great library at Louvain. I continued to feel distant from and not in harmony with the crowd at school. The climax came when in a drawing lesson we were asked to draw a sea battle as we imagined it to be. All went to work feverishly including myself. I drew – as best as I could – several ships, clouds of smoke, sailors on board and also in the water. There was a German flag on one ship and a British one on the other. When a girl looked over my shoulder; and found that I had drawn sailors in the water on the German side, she shouted abuse at me, saying that only English sailors were drowned. The class was ready to lynch me, with wild cries of: *Gott strafe England*, the fashionable slogan against the one-time 'blood brother'. I became frightened, shouting frantically: 'If only English sailors were drowned Emmy's father would not have been killed.' Emmy was a classmate whose father had been a casualty during the first days of the war, and the sad girl, clothed in black, had deeply impressed me. There was silence after my outbreak, then the teacher put her arm round me, and found it expedient to see me home that day. This was something special at a school where contact between teachers and pupils was very formal.

The first wounded soldiers soon arrived, and military hospitals were set up in large houses and in one of the Prince's castles on the periphery of the town. The park was ideal for the convalescent, and a little episode in it stands out in my memory. Mother had sent me with a basket full of fruit, flowers and cigarettes to the hospital. I was to go all by myself, and I dreaded it. However, a nurse took me by the hand, and led me into the gardens where on chairs and camp-beds many soldiers lay in the warm sunshine. They were friendly and gentle, but the sight of bandages, of armless and legless men distressed me, and I was about to run away, when suddenly a man with one arm shouted: 'Come along, *Kleine* – little one – and put a cigarette in my mouth. I haven't had one for months.' Very shyly I approached him. Cigarettes then had gilt tips, and believing these to be ornamental, I put the cigarette into the man's mouth the wrong way round. Everybody laughed but the cigarette was soon changed into its proper position and lit. I was thoroughly glad when my basket was empty, and went home in a hurry.

The horrors of war had touched me visibly.

The effects of war made themselves felt increasingly in our daily lives. Butter, bread, meat, all kinds of food were in short supply, and even the substitutes which the chemists conjured up were hard to come by. The word *Ersatz* became common in our vocabulary. We lived in a rural area, and were better off than many, but our part of the country was invaded by crowds from the densely populated industrial regions who came on *Hamsterfahrten* – excursions on which to collect provisions, and then hoard them, as the hamster does. We ourselves had to go out to farms to see what we could get. Equipped with bags and baskets Mother and I walked for miles to make sure of something to eat. I enjoyed these walks through woods and fields, then to be welcomed in a farmhouse, to have a chat, drink glasses of fresh milk, and perhaps be allowed the freedom of the garden to pick a large bunch of flowers. Later, when things became even scarcer, and potatoes, flour and a bottle of cooking-oil were sought-after treasures, we travelled as far afield as my mother's old home. There she had one or two friends married to farmers, and one to the owner of a mill where they extracted oil from rape seed. We tramped for long hours, at times avoiding the country gendarme in case we had collected more than the rationing laws permitted. Our bags and cases full, we returned triumphantly on the train.

School continued much as usual with the odd day off to celebrate a victory, or the class being taken to the woods to collect berries, mushrooms or beechnuts for food to help save precious stocks.

I had become very keen on literature, and liked reading aloud or reciting poems. For special school assemblies or concerts pupils were chosen to recite or sing. One Christmas it was my turn to recite a poem before the assembled school. I was proud and pleased, and my parents fully approved. By this time, it had become a habit for my father to supervise my fairly heavy homework, and answer questions connected with it. He was interested in my reciting, and I spoke the poem to him repeatedly until he liked the rhythm, and believed I brought the words out well. We were actually busy together a night or two before the Assembly when he received a message from the director of my school asking for one of my parents to call at his office. My mother went the next morning, and was informed that members of the Jewish community had objected to my being involved in a Christmas celebration. He wished to have my parents' views. Without even consulting my father, Mother at once said that she saw no reason whatsoever for my not reciting the poem, and that she wished things to go ahead as planned. I was told about the matter, and the incident helped to drive me further away from 'formal' religion.

Before going to sleep at night I often thought of the soldiers in the front line who, I felt sure, must all pray to the same God to protect them. However, I kept those thoughts to myself.

There was no holiday travel during the war. Long summer weeks were spent at the swimming pool, lying for hours in the deep grass by the river reading. It was then I made the acquaintance of Sherlock Holmes, and forgot everything around me over his and Dr Watson's adventures. Also, I started 'gardening' in large boxes on our balcony, spending contented hours tending tomatoes and radishes. I produced good specimens, and sold them to my mother to increase my pocket money, and so to buy more seeds and plants. I also grew flowers, mainly sweet peas and nasturtiums. As coal became short our winter holidays were doubled and trebled. Schools were heated once a month only, when were given our home tasks for the next few weeks. I used to crowd my work into a few busy days, and then feel gloriously free to go tobogganing in the daytime and have long evenings reading. It was all done on a monotonous diet of cabbage, potatoes, black bread and turnip jam. When I came home desperately hungry out of the crisp winter air our good Marie had often kept, as a special treat, a slice of bread and turnip jam for me 'off the ration'. Her mother on the farm was able to bake 'black' – that is to say from flour kept aside from deliveries the farm had to make to an official depot – and Marie secured a loaf now and then on Sunday visits. Milk was skimmed and looked blueish, and I had to stand in a long queue to get it. Sometimes we were fortunate to get 'real' milk fresh from the farm. This was a black market deal, and Marie and I fetched the milk in a flask in the early hours of the morning or after dark.

The winter of 1916/17 was perhaps the worst for cold, darkness and inadequate food. Clothing, too, was difficult to come by, and I had to wear some horrible dresses made from old and far too heavy curtains. I looked like a dumpy little bell, but I was not alone in this. There were a good few oddities walking about, and looks did not matter much as long as we were reasonably warm. Shoes had to last a long time even when they cramped growing feet, and were not resistant to sleet and slushy snow. Chilblains abounded.

Always small and thin, I became thinner and thinner, and in the early summer of 1917 I went down with a mysterious illness. We had been on a long walk when I complained of sickness, and then literally collapsed into bed on coming home. I soon ran a temperature, became very weak, was constantly thirsty but could not touch food. The doctor was puzzled and my parents worried. They sat by my bedside, holding my hand in turn, calming me when I was delirious. I was later told that I often screamed, so I must have had nightmares during those troubled feverish nights. But I only remember one recurring vision which became familiar and for which I waited with a kind of pleasant anticipation. There appeared in front of me a very large moon which smiled at me, then grew pale blue, bigger and bigger, and eventually burst. After that I had a little uneasy sleep.

One morning after a very bad night, I had been in bed for some weeks now, and there was little left of me, spots appeared on my face, arms and hands. My mother ran for the doctor, and it was confirmed that the measles 'had come out', and that I would probably now get better slowly. My recovery was very, very slow, and I was allowed to return to school only after the long summer holidays which meant being away from school till well into the autumn. It was hoped that sun and fresh air would help to bring back strength.

As soon as I was able to walk a little, Father and I left for the woods close by, morning after morning. The electric tramcar would convey us to a village from which we could easily and quickly reach a quiet place among heather and birch plantations. There we stayed for the rest of the day, living on the food Mother packed for us. And we read, piles and piles of books, in perfect peace. Also, we would talk, and I loved both. During these long tranquil hours Father revealed his true self to me. Life, he said, was full of what he called 'fireworks' but true contentment lay only in work, work enjoyed and work well done. I always sensed a sadness that he had not been allowed to do the work he might have chosen for himself. He was an ardent believer in all the humane virtues, detesting violence in any form, and fervently wishing for peace. He was a true citizen of the world, before it became fashionable to be one. He considered the knowledge of languages an absolute necessity towards gaining understanding among nations. During my unexpectedly long vacation Father added to the little knowledge of French I already had. We read Perrault's *Contes*, and he taught me some French songs and rhymes, often miming the actions to make me understand more easily. With Father I began English, and with the help of a German translation we worked our way through *Little Lord Fauntleroy*, its sweet sentimentality fitting my languid state of convalescence.

I went back to school in the autumn, still pretty weak, my usually thick dark hair thin and limp. I remember the feeling of everything being an effort with not enough energy to keep alert during lessons. I was given a tonic, a thick blood-red syrup which I detested. Also, the doctor decided that I should be exempt from the non-essential subjects, gymnastics, singing and needlework, to allow for extra rest and living – whenever possible – in the open air.

Fresh air in those days was thought of as a substitute for food of which there was so little. I did not mind missing lessons that I did not greatly care for. I was not good at singing or needlework, and I did not like organised gymnastics. There was, however, a great disappointment. My father with his very German respect for academic achievement, and love for the classical languages, had promised to let me have private lessons in Greek and Latin. This might at the same time help to prepare me for university entrance. Preparation in Greek and Latin was necessary in addition to the

Modern Languages of the normal Lyzeum curriculum. The doctor did not now consider me fit enough to cope with the extra work. I felt miserable and disappointed.

A year dragged on wearily with little cheer. The effects of malnutrition became more and more obvious, particularly during a terrible 'flu epidemic when several parents and grandparents of young friends died. In our family I was the only one not to succumb to the infection. Horrified and trembling, lest I should be the only survivor, I carried hot milk to the bedrooms of parents, aunt and maids. My mother was the first to recover and together we nursed the rest back to health. School was closed for a few weeks and when it reopened teachers and pupils seemed weak and depressed, hardly able to carry on with the daily round. Even my once chauvinistic classmates were less aggressive and did not sport black-white-and red bows on their dresses. War seemed no longer heroic as a feeling of hopelessness spread. The grown-ups wondered how long Germany could hold out with her allies weakening and the enemy more formidable through America's involvement. 'Fight until victory' became less likely with the masses longing for peace and an undercurrent of rebellious ideas infiltrating from Russia.

People began to whisper about 'the end' and revolution. Then, early in November 1918, I was at a piano lesson when we suddenly heard guns firing. From the window we discovered that guns had been placed on the roof-tops of barracks almost opposite, and excited crowds thronged the streets below. Everything happened so quickly that we were more startled than frightened. We just switched off the lights and sat quietly in the dark, hoping for the noise to stop. It did after some two hours. Just then our maid, Marie, came up the stairs. Disobeying my parents' orders, she had made her way through the quiet backstreets to get 'the child' home safely through the unknown terrors of revolution. We walked back without any trouble and Marie delivered me to my greatly relieved parents. Obviously they had been much more worried than I or even my music teacher, rumours being more frightening than the real thing.

But revolution it was.

Unrest, begun in the navy, swept through the country within days. Morale in the armed forces and at home collapsed, and the false notion of war being heroic vanished completely. Soldiers' and Workers' Councils took over, the *Kaiser* was forced to abdicate, and with the Crownprince sought refuge in Holland. The rule of our Prince, as that of all rulers of small German states, came to an end too. But there was no bloodshed, and some sort of settlement was agreed upon quickly, while many a loyal subject shed a secret tear. The family of the Prince was well loved.

Although there was no excessive violence in our town, confusion was great, and at school lessons were cancelled for a few days. Instead we were set to making paper flowers which were stuck into small bunches of pine, to be given to soldiers returning from the front. It was explained to us that the German armies had not actually been beaten in the field, but that 'circumstances' had beaten them. The myth of the 'stab in the back' was thus created at once.

We were marched to the railway station, carrying baskets of our home-made dcecorations. Somewhat disheartened bands played on the platform, and I, like most children, felt thoroughly embarrassed when lots of tired disillusioned soldiers arrived who obviously did not want to have anything to do with our silly posies. They did not even smile at the Red Cross ladies who offered them cups of some *Ersatz* brew, but just gulped the stuff down. At least it was hot, and the weather was cold and damp. Many soldiers had torn off their cockades and shoulder pieces, wearing bits of red ribbon instead. Some had red armbands. I clearly remember a man in a torn uniform spitting at our flowers. We were all glad when the 'patriotic reception' was not repeated and school went on as before.

Chapter 5

News of the armistice came on 11th November. Nothing was quite as before, and school continued to be in a somewhat confused state. Apparently orders were given to change the angle of much of the teaching, but naturally there were no new textbooks yet. Many lessons had to be improvised, and depended on the individual stand each teacher took towards the situation. The word democracy was bandied about, and everybody clung to it as to a life-raft in rough waters. A special subject, *Bürgerkunde*, instruction in citizenship, was introduced, and an eager young teacher tried to set out the aims of the brand-new German Republic: liberty and goodwill were written in large letters, and war was outlawed. The end of an epoch, in fact.

Daily life was difficult, with strikes, and shortages of almost everything, and a growing clandestine market kept going by people known as *Schieber*, who 'pushed' goods in order to make an excessive profit. Things became more and more expensive, a great worry in a household depending on a fixed income. Many of my father's foreign investments were 'frozen' or even useless as a result of the war. Strict savings had to be introduced, and when our good Marie married a returned soldier, she was not replaced. Mother now worked with a daily woman only. My dresses and coats were made from clothes sent by my Dutch cousins. Our family had a long connection with Holland, and these relatives were to prove good and helpful friends in those hard years. Through them I had a unique experience.

Though no passports for foreign travel were available to German adults, more and more *Kriegskinder*, children under fourteen, who had suffered in the war years, were sent for holidays to neutral countries. This travel was arranged through organisations like the Quakers – who also provided extra food for thousands of children – or through personal contacts. One of my classmates had been to Scandinavia, and had come back with tales of peace and plenty. It was to be my turn now. A cousin had made preparations for me to spend a couple of months in Holland. I had never quite overcome the weakness caused by my long illness two years earlier. Special leave from school was obtained, and one fine summer's morning my cousin collected me in an elegant dark-blue Packard complete with smart chauffeur. The farewell was a little tearful as I had never been away from my parents for any length of time. However, excitement soon took the upper hand, and I gave myself completely to the new and thrilling experience. For the first time I crossed a frontier, and after the German customs, we soon reached the Dutch maréchausée men, looking well-fed, and in much better uniforms than their German counterparts. They waved us on, and gave the 'war child' a big smile.

The weeks that followed were like a dream. I was given a room on the first floor of my cousin's handsome house. Large glass doors opened on to a big square balcony, the roof of the garden-room below. The garden with flowers, lawns and fruit trees, stretched a long way down till it met the gardens of houses in a street running parallel with ours. At seven o'clock each morning a maid in a cotton dress and white apron came in to draw the curtains, open the balcony doors, and let me enjoy the view. I was served with hot chocolate, and told to rest for another hour or two. Then came breakfast with the family which included cheese, eggs and cold meats, foods I had almost forgotten about, and some I had never seen before, like Dutch honeycake and delicious currant bread. Relations vied to make me strong and happy, and there was a succession of outings and parties. The family owned a farm outside the town, and there we went on hot afternoons by carriage or car, to lounge, to take tea in the open, help with berry picking, or play tennis which I was taught. At weekends we went further afield, and I saw much of the northeast of Holland: picturesque towns and villages, windmills, canals, big flower markets, and men and women wearing *klompjes*, the traditional wooden clogs.

Above all else I lived in a country which had not known war, and where there was great prosperity. Sometimes I found it all a little overwhelming, and in spite of all the comfort and luxury I occasionally longed for home and my parents. I felt from their regular letters that they, too, were missing me.

At the end of two months – we were to leave on a Monday morning – the door bell suddenly rang latish on Sunday night. To everybody's amazement there stood my mother. She had longed for me badly, and impatiently had set out by train to see if a frontier official would give her permission to enter Holland just for one night. She had succeeded, and our joy was great. She was given a huge meal which she could not really enjoy after all the severe rationing.

Next morning we all left by car, laden with presents of food, and I was wearing my first pair of new shoes, a fact I was immensely proud of. For years I had had nothing but shoes handed down to me from someone or other. I had put on several stone, and my hair had gone back to its normal thickness and shine. I was grateful yet happy and anxious to get home. Two months' separation from my father and mother, in a new and foreign country, had changed me in some strange way.

Physically and mentally I was different.

Childhood was over. The journey to Holland was a watershed. The thirteen-year-old child was growing into a young woman of almost fourteen.

In some ways life at school had also changed. Equality for women was much talked about, influenced possibly by echoes from revolutionary Russia, and now propagated by German Marxist writers. Women were to take a more active part in society. To be prepared for their new role, they must receive an education equal to that of boys. Even our half-comprehending minds became filled with new and exciting ideas.

Science gained greater importance in our curriculum. Fortunately for me who just scraped through mathematics and science subjects, the arts held their place with the teaching of the history and appreciation of art as important subjects. We were encouraged to form and express opinions and write essays on topics which appealed to us. I had developed a great liking for the Italian Renaissance painters, and I happily spent long hours with Vasari's *Lives of the Italian Painters*. The book's story-telling style brought the period very close, and I eventually wrote an essay full of definite views on the painters and the Renaissance as a whole.

Teachers no longer addressed us by the familiar *Du*, but used the formal *Sie*, though still with our first names. This meant a lot to us, showing, as it did, that we were no longer considered 'children'. To be called *gnädiges Fräulein* in some shop or other, was honey to my ears. I so desperately wanted to be grown-up.

Clothes were a great hindrance to this ambition. With material and money – prices kept rising – in very short supply, we just had to go on wearing clothes as long as they would hang together. I remember crying my eyes out when I had to go to a party dressed in an old blouse, white with blue sailor's collar; quite smart at one time, but now, I thought, beneath contempt.

Again help came from our good relations in Holland. On every visit they brought bundles of new clothes. Old they may have been to them, they were treasure-trove to me and a few friends who benefited from the largesse. I was never good at sewing, but I enjoyed sitting evening after evening unpicking dresses, suits and skirts. In the end my mother booked a week with the home-dressmaker. Much sought after, she was a very genteel lady, commanding respect from everybody. She only worked, it was said for 'good families', and she did work well. When eventually the appointed date came along the *Fräulein* would arrive complete with her small sewing machine and a clean white overall to put over her neat dress. My mother had the 'sewing room' ready, with a large table for cutting and boxes of thread of all colours, cotton and silk. All week Mother was prepared to be the dressmaker's assistant, doing the hand-finishing, bits of embroidery or decorative stitching which might be required. By the time I came home from school, they would be well established, and with some luck I could try on their first 'creation'. It was astonishing what marvellous clothes could be made from cast-offs. I achieved my great desire: a 'tailor-made', a handsome little suit, a symbol then for being 'grown-up'. Navy-blue it was, with a pale-blue silk shirt tucked into the skirt.

Apart from her undoubted success in conjuring up 'new' clothes, the dressmaker was a welcome visitor for the pleasant gossip – never malicious – and tales she brought with her. At meals which she shared, and during the early evening hours, my homework done, I listened eagerly to tongues going as quickly as the needles. During fittings, too, when the dressmaker sometimes knelt on the floor to 'sort a hem', as she called it, she would suddenly remove a pin which she held precariously between her lips and begin one of her stories. No longer young, she had known the court in its heyday. Fancy, she having been among a number of dressmakers who, with the help of personal maids, of course, had dressed great ladies, yes, even princesses, for the Court Ball. And what is more, she told me, 'your own grandfather supplied some of the material for the dresses, and gorgeous they were. At one time he had to get long kid gloves straight from the Tyrol, dyed to tone with the dresses.' Most of the dresses, she explained, had trains which the ladies carried gracefully slung over one arm when they walked up the wide carpeted stairs to the ballroom in the Prince's palace. Notwithstanding the 'new spirit', and our democratic enthusiasms, princely glamour still held its attractions.

Among the Dutch 'seconds' there was a left-over piece of blue and pink printed crêpe de chine which made a longish Russian-type smock. Worn over my blue skirt, this became my first evening outfit, and I was proud of it. Something to wear in the evening had now become important as passion for the theatre was growing with me and my friends. Everybody then dressed for the occasion. In fact, visits to the theatre were social events. Though our pocket-money would only stretch to seats high up in the gallery, we hurried in the interval to the foyer below, to see and perhaps be seen. Some slightly older boys, with whom we had a nodding acquaintance, had reached the independence of earning money of their own. They could afford the luxury of the dress circle and we enjoyed being seen by them in our finery. We used our scant resources to buy the cheapest seats as often as possible. Our tastes were catholic: the German classics, Shakespeare, Molière, Strindberg and Ibsen in translation, Gerhart Hauptmann, Wedekind and, of course, Toller and the early Brecht caught our imagination. We identified with the characters, particularly in modern plays, questioned and even accused the past, in favour of a stirring present and what we liked to think of as a 'fabulous future'. Yet, romance still had a grip on us, and we were thrilled by the gaiety of *Die Fledermaus* and *The Merry Widow*, while *Lilac Time*, the sentimental story of Schubert's life, made us shed copious tears.

In spite of the many worries of our elders, to us, the young, life in the new Weimar Republic seemed good. We felt the excitement of a fresh beginning. And to be young and fully experiencing the advent of a new epoch was important, at least that is what we thought. We were keen and we were curious. The Austrian count Coudenhove-Kalerghi's thoughts on *Pan-Europa*, a united Europe, had the admiration of a generation who fervently believed in the clarion call of *Nie wieder Krieg*: United States of Europe, we thought, was a logical step to take, ending the frontiers of countries in the same way German principalities had ended. After all, there had been a time when Hessians thought themselves completely different from, say, the people of Hamburg and Hanover, as the French might now do from the Germans or British. But though individual differences remained and were distinct, internal German frontiers had fallen, and no longer was a passport with seven or eight visas required for someone from Westphalia to travel to the south of Germany. This had still been necessary in the mid-nineteenth century, and my father – a strong *Pan-European* – kept just such a passport which had belonged to his own father.

The study of languages was steadily gaining in importance, a step nearer to becoming 'European'. I had always liked French and English, and now devoted more and more time to acquiring a degree of fluency. Father with his very good knowledge of languages was a wonderful companion in my quest. We arranged for me to spend an hour every evening in his study, aiming at speaking one evening only English and the next French.

During these evenings a curious little incident happened to which, I believe, I owe my capacity of having stayed all through life a one or two cigarettes-a-day woman.

The slightly older and hence very superior-feeling brother of a schoolmate of mine kept boasting that he enjoyed smoking. He came in one day when his sister was spending the afternoon with me, and grandly supplied us with a cigarette each. He then dared us to smoke them at once. We had just lit them, and were awkwardly puffing and coughing when my father came home from a walk. To put it mildly, we were thunderstruck. However, all Father said quite casually was, 'Carry on, I hope you won't be sick.'

Next day when I entered his study for our conversation hour, he asked how I had enjoyed the smoke. 'It's fine', I answered, with more boast than truth, after which Father pointed to a small metal box on his desk, filled with Turkish cigarettes. He was a pipe smoker with the occasional cigar after dinner, but kept cigarettes for his visitors. I had for long been fascinated by the tin box in which these cigarettes were packed, less for its contents than the coloured picture of an Oriental market on its slightly rounded lid. It had all the magic of the Arabian nights.

Now Father opened the lid, saying, 'Please take one,' and with a gallant gesture lit my cigarette, adding, 'as for me, I have nothing against smoking, within reason, that is. But what I do not want you to do, is smoke in secret.' After that the tin box was offered to me every evening. The nightly cigarette became a pleasant ritual in the same way a glass of half wine, half water, with dinner had been since infancy. It is as well to remember that a very drinkable table wine, red or white, then cost something in the region of twenty pence a bottle. I took Father's order to the local wine merchant two or three times a year, and several hundred bottles arrived a day or two after, to be stored on the shelves of the wine cellar. Mulled wine was a regular party drink though, as I was to find out later, for the young some strong tea was added to the spicy mixture.

There were frequent smallish parties now where we gathered to talk about everything under the sun. We met in each other's houses and chatted and chatted, though ten o'clock was the very latest time for getting home, a rule kept strictly and never questioned.

Next to the theatre, art was our great interest. Small exhibitions introduced us to what was going on in the great world outside. We saw and we marvelled. Pictures and sculptures were so different from what we had been shown in lessons and on the odd visit to museums and galleries we had paid a memorable visit to nearby Kassel and the sumptuous Baroque of parks and palaces had delighted us. But what we now saw was new and closer to our own world, we felt. Somebody organised lectures on Expressionism and Dadaism. They were a revelation, and Dada became our god. This was at a time when dreams and the subconscious had become respectable. Sigmund Freud began making an impact on us, and ideas on 'complex' and 'repression' came down to us from older friends.

When the painter-poet Kurt Schwitters returned to his native Hanover, we saved for weeks to be able to travel – fourth class, of course – to hear the master read his poems in weirdly decorated rooms. We saw his collages of used railway tickets, bits of sacking, string and other odds and ends, and recognised them as works of art, which they certainly were. Through Schwitters we became acquainted with the drawings of Georges Grosz, acidly exposing the stuffiness of bourgeois life and arrogant militarism which we fervently believed dead forever. We did not realise then that an ever growing reaction was working against the young German republic whose politicians they held responsible for accepting the 'Dictate of Versailles'.

Meantime we attended concerts of modern music, and in candle-lit bookshops listened to poetry which to our surprise did not rhyme.

Boys now loomed larger in our lives, even if only in a very platonic way. Sex was never talked about either at school or at home, but friendships between boys and girls were taken for granted and not discouraged. It is perhaps strange in the present-day climate that nowhere was there ever any reference made to the physical side of relationships. I had long since outgrown the stork stories which I was told in plenty when I was very young. I then firmly believed in them, to the point of putting out lumps of sugar to attract the baby-carrying bird to the window, and leave the brother I would have dearly loved to have. Nothing ever replaced the stork tales, and what I did learn were facts gleaned here and there, from schoolmates and older friends who felt very important in being able to enlighten the lesser fry. These bits and pieces were assembled like a jigsaw puzzle without ever putting questions to our parents. I am sure they would have been dreadfully embarrassed by them anyway. Somehow I did not worry, and the implicit rules of behaviour created neither complex nor frustration to limit the enjoyment of life, with me, at least.

Many of my friends belonged to *Wandervogel*. Begun before the First World War as an association of young people who sought recreation in simple things: folksong, music, country dancing and hiking, this particular youth movement had come to mean a way of life. It meant the rejection of materialism and expediency, artificiality and the increasing mechanisations of existence. Natural joy was set against the pursuit of sophisticated pleasures, honesty against hypocrisy. The conscience of the individual was to be the deciding factor in any situation. It all sounds very modern, yet it was the acknowledged creed of great numbers of young people more than fifty years ago. Indeed, I believe that much of the movement's thought content lives on in progressive education and even in the 'folk' revivals of our own day. The American judge Lindsay's books on 'comradeship marriages' were applauded, and I surprised my mother by airing the unconventional thought that I should hate to wake up one morning next to a near-stranger, and would much prefer to know somebody well before I committed myself for life. My forebearing mamma just smiled and, of course, the conventions we were brought up in, did not allow for more than slight flirtations. These were indulged in and greatly enjoyed.

I had reached my last year at school and was working hard for the Lyzeum's Leaving Certificate which set a high standard. I still hoped that a way might be found for me to go to university, though it would mean a further two years' training at the boys' *Gymnasium*. Just then classmates began talking about dancing lessons, and from a reluctant father and a more sympathetic mother I gained permission to take part in the winter session of the dancing school. Some thirty boys met as many girls twice a week on the parqueted dance floor of the red-plush-and-chandeliers ballroom of a local hotel. The tall and elegant dancing master explained the steps, and then with his 'tails' flying, produced them alone or sometimes with his equally tall and elegant wife.

The boys in the row facing us were very awkward, and there were many giggles from the girls before the opposite sex responded. The first shyness gone, it all became great fun. When at last our end-of-term dance came along, with paper streamers and coloured balloons, we excelled in quick-steps, foxtrots and tangos. The waltz was still a great favourite, and no formal ball began without a polonaise when every boy presented his partner with a corsage of flowers to be worn proudly for the rest of the night. To receive just one purple orchid, surrounded by feathery fern, its stem protected by silver foil, was the height of delight. It was customary for parents to accompany their sons and daughters to the ball. They sometimes joined in the dancing but spent most of the evening in a room next to the dance floor, playing cards or just making polite conversation. After a light meal during the late evening our elders left, to allow us half an hour to be 'walked home' by our partners. A handkiss at our own front door made a romantic ending to the night's innocent excitement.

That winter the purchasing power of the mark dwindled

alarmingly as more and more paper money was being printed. It then became clear to my father that for me a university education was out of the question. There were no grants, and galloping inflation and forever shrinking reserves harshly shattered my dreams of becoming a student. I should have to look for work to which the ten-year Lyzeum course fitted me. I was disappointed and even wept myself to sleep at night. Yet, I tried to hide my feelings as Father himself was depressed enough over a decision forced upon him. Together with many parents of his own age group he saw his savings melt away, and I will never forget him saying sadly over and over again: 'I'll end up a beggar after a lifetime of work.' Some twenty years older than my mother, he was not now young and fit enough to begin all over again. Salaried people did not feel the pinch so badly as their earnings rose with the ever increasing cost of living.

In the spring of 1922 most young people leaving High School in Germany looked for work in an office, with banks being special favourites. Close to the source of information, even boys and girls with little money speculated against the mark, investing in foreign currency whenever possible. Many of these 'bankers' spent money copiously, dressing better than the rest of us, eating in expensive places, and the young men chasing about on motor bikes, mostly with a girl on the pillion seat. There was great competition for becoming a *Klammerbraut* a bride, – girlfriend would be the better interpretation – who had to hang on tightly to her man.

I spent many anxious hours, wondering what career to follow. I still found it hard to put that 'student image' out of my mind. Industry or commerce did not attract me. Then, in a sudden flash, I knew that to train as a bookseller, and work among books, would be the nearest thing to a university education now denied me. In some ways, more even than I suspected at the time, it was a business career, yet it was different.

Father, in a pessimistic mood, was doubtful of my ambitions. The time was not far away, he thought, when nobody would be able to afford books, and bookseller's apprentices were mostly boys anyway. However, I knew of at least one girl who was training, and

I persisted. Mother, as usual more positive, was willing to help and did procure me an interview with the town's leading bookseller-cum-publisher.

The great man gave me a lecture on the hard work required during years of careful training, with quite a lot of manual labour which I would be expected to do just like 'the other boys'. This was, of course, if I were to be accepted at all. He would give the matter his careful consideration once he had received a report on my scholastic achievements. I was not dismayed by the interview as I had liked my possible future boss at first sight.

One fine day in April the big doors of the girls' High School closed behind me, and that very day a letter arrived accepting me as an apprentice into the firm which had been printers, publishers, and booksellers for over two hundred and fifty years. I was to acquire a solid knowledge of the booktrade and of the complicated processes which go into the making of a book. I should learn how to edit manuscripts, read proofs, and be introduced to the world of journalism, with the prospect of free theatre and cinema tickets, if I showed any talent for reviewing. I might even get some reporting to do.

I would earn very little – particularly with ever increasing inflation – and would not be able to contribute to the costs of the household. Yet I was assured of an excellent free training and could live at home.

I was jubilant and full of eager anticipation. My parents were glad to see me happy, although both, particularly my father, still felt secretly sad that they could not now give me some years at university.

Regulations concerning the training of apprentices were very strict. A firm could only employ so many at a time. No vacancy was to occur in my firm until December of the year, and I had to contain my eagerness for all these months to come. What was I to do all summer and autumn? We could not afford the still fashionable *Pension für junge Mädchen*, a sort of minor Finishing School, nor did the idea of being cooped up with some twenty girls, for no real purpose, appeal to me.

My future boss sent me a pile of books on printing, the history of the booktrade and similar subjects, which I began reading avidly, taking notes for keeping in loose-leaf booklets. Then came an invitation from one of my mother's younger brothers for me to spend six months with his family in Hamburg. This was a wonderful opportunity. Everybody knew Hamburg to be a cosmopolitan city, a window on the wide world.

My uncle, his pretty wife and three young sons lived in a fine house with a large garden stretching down to one of the many waterways of the *Aussen-Alster*, part of Hamburg's river which widens out into two famous lakes. Overwhelmed with new impressions, I drank it all in: the wealth, the elegance and the sheer size – to me at least – of the city and its great port. My uncle was in the oil business which even then was lucrative and ever growing. He took me to his downtown offices and sometimes on inspection tours of tankers in the port. In a small launch we splashed between forests of masts, and saw ocean-going giants being piloted to the mouth of the Elbe. The harbour area was crowded with people of all colours and many races, and this whiff of the great world excited me. So did the water itself. Having lived hundreds of miles inland, I only knew quiet rivers and the odd sleepy lake in the woods and I will never forget my first sight of the sea at Cuxhaven. My aunt introduced me to other new worlds: the city's luxurious shops and the smart shopping crowds which assembled for elevenses in the *Alsterpavillon*, an exquisite café overlooking the Alster in the centre of Hamburg's promenade, the *Jungfernstieg*. I was taken to St. Pauli to see the nightlife of the *Reeperbahn*, at least its milder manifestations. We visited hippodromes where for a few marks one could ride round under the spotlights to martial music, to be 'handed down' by one of the riding masters who all looked like surplus officers from the K. and K. Austrian army. We saw *Maskottchen*, a high-spirited musical, a nautical tale whose catchy tunes were heard everywhere in this nautical city. I was taken to a small *Tanzbar* where cabaret alternated with the tiny floor being cleared for the clientele to dance on. We sat on high stools drinking Sherry Cobblers from frosted glasses. Hot chicken soup, served after midnight, was the signal for going home.

I found my way quickly around the city. When I was not sharing my cousins' games, helping in house or garden or exploring my uncle's library, I admired, open-mouthed, the many wonders of Hamburg: buildings, parks, galleries and museums. But not all was wonder. In the old parts of the city – which had survived the great fire in 1842 – I saw slums, poverty which I never dreamt could exist. In my little town nobody was excessively rich and nobody was distressingly poor either. Here contrasts were great when only half a mile away from the glitter of the *Jungfernstieg* were nasty dark and damp courtyards where thin, pale children played among heaps of rubbish. Only now did I understand some modern poetry which I had read without really fully understanding it. The sound and rhythm of Arno Holz had appealed to me, but I never quite knew what he meant by *Vorstadtelend*. Now I knew that there did exist whole districts of cities given to misery and decay. For the first time I sensed the social problems created by large cities and an industrial society.

For July and August my uncle had taken a house in Westerland on Sylt. The whole household, including cook, nanny and chambermaid, were to travel by rail and then boat to the small island off the coast of Slesvig Holstein. This promised another great adventure.

Just before our departure our joy was much dampened by the news of the callous murder of Germany's Foreign Minister, Walther Rathenau. Disregarding his many achievements, he was shot down by right-wing extremists while on his way to the *Reichstag*. Together with other politicians he was blamed for what was called 'the shameful dictate of Versailles', and, what is more, he was a Jew, and the anti-semitic campaign was growing in Germany. The term, 'Jewish pig' was bandied about quite openly. The Weimar government passed a law 'for the protection of the Republic', a not very effective gesture, as it would prove.

That autumn, too, Mussolini's Blackshirts took Italy by storm – the first rumblings of the earthquake to come.

Chapter 6

I returned to my parents wiser for the experience but once again contented to get back to our more simple and quiet way of life.

A couple of months went by quickly, and the first of December arrived in no time. It was a cold and frosty morning with the stars still bright in the sky when my life as a bookseller began. I had badly wanted a new dress for the great occasion but there was no earthly chance of getting one. However, inventive as always, my mother had produced a fine light cashmere suit from her pre-war wardrobe. Unpicked and dyed navy blue, it was fashioned into a smart shirtwaister, the almost standard 'uniform' for entering what was still considered a man's world. The only thing new in this outfit were two sets of white piqué collar and cuffs; two, because the dusty atmosphere of a bookshop would make frequent changes necessary.

My working day was from eight o'clock in the morning to seven o'clock at night, with two hours off for lunch. There were neither half days nor tea breaks. As the youngest apprentice I had to start half an hour earlier, to collect the mail from the post office, all but parcels. I was handed the key to the post box and a huge leather bag. Filled to the top, it was almost as big as myself, and I struggled along under the weight of letters and printed matter, coping with the first task of my morning routine. The mail had to be on the boss's desk at 8 o'clock prompt every morning. My new way of life held many surprises, and was by no means the literary haven of my dreams.

Parcels had to be unpacked, with the brown paper carefully folded for reuse and string, not cut, but unknotted and rewound. Stoves all over the place, laid the night before by the cleaners, had to be lit, and woe was me if they smoked. I had never lit a stove before but it was all new experience and exciting in that way. Urgent letters in the town or even piles of books, for some reason or other not entrusted to the porters, had to be delivered by me. When there was snow on the ground, the books were tied to a toboggan which I pulled uphill, looking forward to the moment when I could slide down on the empty sledge.

However, I also had many hours of more serious training. I was disappointed when my boss decided that my first four or five months should be spent not in the bookshop but in the firm's head office. He explained that here, in the nerve centre of the whole enterprise, I would get an understanding of how things were managed, and in time I could face the public with greater confidence and efficiency. In the weeks and months to come I certainly learnt office routine, filing, cataloguing and indexing. I taught myself to type, with two or three fingers albeit, but it has served me well over the years. Also, I was seconded for short periods to the printing and binding departments, and even though I did not do much of the actual work, I found out a lot about the making of a book, the different printing processes and the reading of proofs.

In the spring of 1923 the time had come for me to join the bookshop staff, and just then a disturbing incident exposed the working of reactionary and dangerous forces, and the way they could influence an individual's life.

One of the young booksellers, employed by the firm, flatly refused to work beside 'someone of non-Aryan blood'. There had been heated discussions behind closed doors, before I was acquainted with the 'facts'. The young man had apparently calmed down, and I assured my boss that I was unconcerned although deep down the situation embarrassed me. In fact, the man left the firm soon afterwards, not before apologising for any rumours I might have heard. Pathetically he explained that a 'club' he belonged to had fed him on anti-semitic literature, and though he was not sure whether he had ever met a Jew, he felt it was his duty to protest.

In 1923 this was proof of the early effect on the minds of people of propaganda spread by the new National Socialist party. According to their vicious doctrine the Jews were held responsible for the lost war and its aftermath. ' Pure Aryans' only could lead Germany back to greatness. When French troops occupied the Rhineland and the industrial region of the Ruhr, staging a show of strength in order to demand the fulfilment of the terms of the Peace Treaty, militant nationalism grew. There was massive resistance, and heroes of the resistance were created. Martyrs, such as Albert Leo Schlageter, shot by order of the French occupation, later entered the Nazi mystique. In the same year Adolf Hitler's abortive coup heightened tensions.

Many Germans not infatuated with the struggling Weimar Republic, began nostalgically to look back on a 'glorious' past, particularly the armed forces. The *Reichswehr*, the country's limited army, brought back officers who had served under the *Kaiser*. Quasi-military associations of war veterans marched through the streets, chanting offensive slogans, often confronting each other in bloody fights, while, it was said, police looked the other way.The extreme right-wing *Stahlhelm*, with many ex-officers in its midst, was fiercely opposed to the left-orientated *Reichsbanner*, devoted to the black-red-and-gold flag of the Republic. These colours chosen to represent the liberal spirit of the ill-fated 1848 German Assembly,were now openly rejected. The imperial black-white-and-red was again sported by would-be patriots. Communism, strong in the larger cities and the industrial parts of Germany was the dreaded and menacing spectre. Wherever members of the extreme Left met, they were blasted with shouts of '*Blut muss fliessen*' – we want blood – by their political opponents.

The men of the Weimar Republic failed to put an end to the menace.

With the professional and middle classes, depression and discontent increased as their poverty grew. There was a wave of suicides, particularly among the elderly who felt unable to cope. The chasm between rich and poor was forever widening. Fortunes were made by speculators who bought up foreign currency or goods which kept increasing in value. *Flucht in den Sachwert* – flight into real estate or durable property – was their slogan. Their womenfolk wore several valuable rings on each finger, and it was rumoured that successful farmers kept grand pianos and fine paintings stored in cowsheds and henhouses.

By the summer of 1923 I had become used to dealing with the public, and after the slightly embarrassed start, I now enjoyed meeting a variety of people. On the whole book buying was then a leisurely business. The professional classes were certainly impoverished, but still had time on their hands. To them a bookshop was a social centre. One browsed, one talked and one might meet some local gentry, even a sprinkling of members of the former ruling family. A good few of the nouveau riche came too, as they were now aspiring to 'culture'.

While many of our customers just came in to browse and buy the odd inexpensive book – all they could afford now – the new rich poured out money like water. Books to them were investment. Also a well-filled bookcase would demonstrate their new status, and help to overcome their deep-seated insecurity which lingered under the brassy surface. Whatever filled the bookcase did not matter in the least, and many a time I or another assistant had to make the choice. 'Well-bound classics' often were asked for. Publishers even cashed in on this trend, one of them advertising – if memory serves me well – '*Goethe, Heine, Schiller, Lessing wertbeständiger sind als Messing*', indicating that these German classics would keep their value better than solid metal. The most startling customer arrived one morning, an industrialist, quickly come to wealth. He had just built an elegant villa for himself and his family, and after having the gardens laid out, he now planned the interior of the house. He acquainted me with the fact that his study needed 'books bound in red and blue leather', to fill some ten metres of shelving. The colours were to match the general décor of the room. Titles were immaterial as long as the colour specification was met. It was and the deal was clinched.

The young were totally different. Some of them, only slightly older than myself, were students, home on vacation from nearby universities. They were a motley crowd, mostly men; only a sprinkling of women. Their politics were of the Left, and they had high hopes for a stable democratic Germany. Keen readers of Marxist literature, they saw in what they called 'the Russian experiment' a chance for the hungry and the oppressed. This young crowd was bright and lively, interested in all that was new and exciting. I made friends of some of them, and many an evening we spent talking literature and art. We discussed the anti-war writers of Europe, all of us having taken a strong stance against militarism. Romain Rolland had our special admiration and René Schickele who, as an Alsatian, was in a particularly strong position to see the absurdity of an ancient enmity between neighbours on both sides of the Rhine. We praised the pacifism of Käthe Kollwitz's stark graphics, and looked with wonder at the activities of the *Bauhaus* and Gropius's New Architecture. The *Neue Sachlichkeit* in building and design was to finish for ever bourgeois pomp and stuffiness.

My friends recommended books to me, books they read at university and others in their spare time, and whole unexpected worlds opened to me. I read about the life of the big city, and again words were put to situations I had observed during my stay in Hamburg – the brilliance and the squalor. Even now there was no squalor in our little town though 'genteel' poverty grew daily as the mark plunged lower and lower on the international exchanges. A piano being loaded on an open farm cart, payment perhaps for a winter supply of potatoes, became a familiar sight. Precious Meissen china, antique silver, all kinds of heirlooms, changed hands for much-coveted eggs, butter and cheese.

Whoever had money spent it quickly because its value was sure to be less on the following day. I well remember turning my apprentice's salary for a month into a quarter of a pound of Gruyère cheese to take home to my mother, after standing in a long queue at the grocer's. She had often longed for this luxury, now available again at a price.

In December 1922 when I began work, one pound sterling was worth about 34.000 marks. By the autumn of 1923 its value had reached an astronomical figure. Savings of a lifetime vanished overnight, and for all those depending on a fixed income, the developments spelt ruin. My father became increasingly depressed, and with our closeness of childhood days remaining strong, he confessed humiliation at having to accept gifts from younger members of my mother's family. 'A beggar after a long life of work,' were words he repeated again and again. 'I did not want you to be a slave,' he often added, referring to my long working days of eight or nine hours. 'I wanted you to go to university, travel, and get a liberal education.' All my assurances that I was happy and did not feel 'a slave' at all, did not drive the sad look from his sensitive face.

In my 'slavery', as Father called it, I had to carry twice a day, often three times, biggish suitcases full of paper money to the post office. The money was sent by telegraph-giro to publishers, together with orders for books. If the money were allowed to stay in the safe even for one night, a hundred books sold one day might buy fifty or fewer only the next. To keep adequate stocks became a nightmare, and a system was invented by which goods were marked at a *Grundpreis*, a basic price, which was multiplied each day by a formula arrived at according to the current value of the mark. Soon this formula had to be changed several times a day.

It seemed like a miracle when in October 1923 Dr. Hjalmar Schacht then president of the *Reichsbank*, produced the *rentenmark*. With it he created a stable currency, guaranteed by real estate and commercial enterprise. Would it be the end of chaos? With the proverbial German orderliness and will to work hard, the way ahead looked brighter. Though this new currency was at first restricted to a few categories of privileged earners, civil servants and the like, every employee was in time paid in *rentenmark*. By December even I could buy two or three good cigars as a Christmas present for my father and a small box of Lindt chocolates for Mother, just carrying a normal purse instead of a bagful of paper notes.

That year the Christmas candles shone like lights at the end of a long dark tunnel.

For some considerable time after the mark had been stabilised it was hard to believe that a thing could be bought week after week for the same price. Turning money at once into goods instead of keeping it to see it dissolve into nothing, had become a habit. To save money and spend it later on something desirable, made sense only gradually.

Ever since an indulging groom in the Prince's stable had let a small girl sit quietly on a bundle of straw, to watch the horses being groomed and harnessed, I had wanted to learn to ride. In fact, I was crazy about horses.

Now came my chance.

In the 1918 revolution the Prince's stud together with the riding school had been nationalised, made into a training centre for professional horsemen, and amateur enthusiasts. I began saving hard earned marks until I had accumulated enough for ten riding lessons. A dashing riding instructor formerly attached to the court, became my teacher. In the elegant riding school we were put through our paces, often being told to look into the mirrors to see that we 'sat like monkeys on a barrel organ'. We were literally taught step by step, and not allowed into the open until we had achieved a reasonable seat and some sort of mastery of our mounts. Supplied by the Prince's stud, they were perfect, often far too good for our capacities.

Ten riding lessons were, of course, not enough to satisfy our instructor's high standards. More marks had to be saved precariously, and more lessons taken until at last I was declared fit to join in an open-air expedition. One Sunday morning we set out for the nearby hills and woodlands, now quite relaxed in the saddle. I can still see in my mind's eye the sunny clearing where I had my first glorious canter. After that we trotted on mossy paths to the Prince's hunting box, turned into a small restaurant, to lunch on Westphalian smoked ham, pumpernickel and a *Steinhäger*, the aquavit of the country. Toasts were drunk to our first successful outing before we turned our horses for home.

At that time, too, I made my first attempt at driving a motor car, an open tourer with the spare wheel strapped to its side. I was supervised by a friend's chauffeur in a smart blue uniform, shining boots and a peaked cap. Under no circumstances would he allow a speed of more than some 10km.p.h. I also started to play tennis regularly. This was possible only by setting my alarm clock for 5 o'clock in the morning, gulping a glass of milk, and then walking half an hour to the courts. We then played till 7 o'clock, and ran home to change and be at work at 8 o'clock prompt. These early hours of tennis were a joint enterprise by members of my firm, and very enjoyable. In general, leisure activities were restricted to evenings and Sundays. Bookselling occupied me fully for the rest of the time.

One day and very unexpectedly I was summoned before the chief. Sitting behind his huge desk he smiled reassuringly, asked me to take a seat, and then told me of his decision to terminate my apprenticeship long before the accepted period of five years. He thought I had learned all there was to learn, and there and then he put me in charge of his bookselling department. I have never known what prompted this sudden and at first rather frightening advancement, and putting me, a girl, barely nineteen years old, into what until then had been a man's place. I could only guess that on the leaving of an older employee, the firm was tempted to save money. I would certainly be cheap although my pay did rise, and I learnt there and then to stand up for women getting the same pay as men, provided they did the same work. However, my age and comparative inexperience kept me in 'the lower grades' meantime. All the same, I did enjoy my new responsibilities, and got on well with those who now worked under me, a few slightly older than myself. My father was proud and delighted. In some way, I suppose, my new standing eased his mind of thoughts of 'slavery'. Always a very quiet man, he had in recent years become more remote, withdrawn into his world of books and music, as an escape from the changing realities of life. During 1924 his eyesight became poor, and even strong glasses did not make the pursuit of his favourite activities easy. He still played the piano well from memory but could not now read for long. Otherwise his health seemed reasonable enough, and he took to having long walks.

It was a bright snowy day in January 1925 when after lunch – I always came home for this meal – he encouraged me to have a walk before returning to work. I accepted eagerly, and hand in hand we walked through the snow chatting as usual. At a corner near my bookshop he proposed to turn back 'as Mother does not like to wait for her coffee.' My parents took their after-lunch-cup always about 3 o'clock, the time I had to be back at work. Father and I parted and, as always, turned a couple of times to wave to each other. Some ten minutes later I received a telephone call at the shop, asking me to come home at once as Father was ill. I said that this must be a mistake; we had just had a walk together. I was told not to argue but hurry home. At that I put on my coat and rushed away to find that my father had collapsed and died in the arms of a policeman on point duty just outside our house. I was numb with grief, and Mother and I lived through the next few days in a ghastly unreal nightmare.

At the end of the week my chief visited us, gently suggesting that to return to work might be a comfort. A relation came to stay for a while with my mother, and I went back to my duties, working mechanically to begin with and quite unable to concentrate. Perhaps to take my mind off the immediate past and also, I believe to test my capacity, my chief informed me that I was to attend the Leipzig Book Fair. He would allow me a substantial sum to buy books for stock, entirely at my own discretion. This was a big assignment and to be able to go to Leipzig seemed a marvellous prospect to a young bookseller who in that city would feel at the centre of her universe. Leipzig's institutions were then a pattern for the booktrade of the world.

Chapter 7

The middle and late twenties saw a flood of exciting books in Germany. With new developments in the graphic arts and a multitude of talent, books attracted the public's attention as objects. Type, printing, layout, binding and dust jackets became the concern of first-class designers. Publishers vied with each other to create a definite visible identity in the books they produced down to the smallest detail, such as the colophon on the title page. Contents, of course, remained of prime importance. The Book Fairs of those years displayed an enormous variety to choose from. Oswald Spengler's *The Decline of Western Civilisation* suited the mood of the times, and created a great deal of discussion. Many writers groped for new ways, trying to sort out the confusion of a society shaken out of its tradition and its established beliefs. The discourses of Count Keyserling's *School of Wisdom*, in Darmstadt and Rudolf Steiner's anthroposophic teachings gave support to many searching for wholeness in an increasingly fragmented existence. Steiner was to have considerable and lasting influence on education. German novelists produced some of their best work. Thomas Mann's *Magic Mountain* appeared in 1924, and Leon Feuchtwanger's world success, *Jew Süss*, in the same year. There was also a spate of excellent translations from many European languages. With no television, and radio only a fringe interest, large numbers of these books were needed to satisfy the reading demand, even in a small town. The greatest bestseller of them all was to be Erich Maria Remarque's *All Quiet on the Western Front*. Through it the civilian came face to face for the first time with the blood, mud and stench of the trenches, and the utter debasement of human values through war. The response to the book was immediate, so that a small-town bookseller could dispose of some 500 copies in a couple of weeks. Disillusion was total, and in this book it had found popular expression. Remarque was only one, if a very powerful one, of many voices speaking out against mass murder and the futility of war. Ludwig Renn's *Krieg* and Henri Barbusse's *Le Feu*, written during the war, and now translated into German, found thousands of readers. War veterans felt that at long last the gap dividing them from those who had remained at home, was narrowing. Robert Cedrick Sherriff's play, *Journey's End*, translated into German as *Die andere Seite*, drew large audiences. When I saw it at our local theatre, the young British soldiers caught in the hell of shell fire, received a standing ovation, accompanied by shouts of '*Nie Wieder Krieg!*' Everywhere anti-war cries were loud and persisting.

In contrast a book written by an obscure Austrian during his detention following an abortive coup, and published in 1925, was largely ignored. *Mein Kampf* was not taken seriously; our bookshop never even stocked it.

With hindsight and in the light of events that followed, this seems stupid and regrettable. Personally, I received a deep hurt from the hatred being stirred up then by National-Socialist ideas. Not long before my father's death I had met a young man, a few years older than myself. Intelligent and very good-looking, he was a young girl's dream. A friendship developed between us, and after he had called on my parents – an absolute necessity in those days – he was accepted as a friend of the family. We went for walks together, visited the theatre or sat over an ice cream at the local pastry shop. In the short time of knowing him, my friend had grown to like my father. Then, in the emotional climate of loss which I am sure he felt too, our friendship grew into love. That is at least what we thought it was.

He was transferred to a new job in another town, and we both suffered the sorrow of parting. However, letters flew backwards and forwards and when that summer my mother and I sought a couple of weeks' rest and change in a remote village of the Alps, my young man followed us there to take his own holiday. It was bliss, as attraction and understanding grew in daily contact. The romantic surroundings also did their bit, and almost unspoken we began to think of a future together. The blow fell a few months later when he told me in a letter that the mere idea of marrying someone of 'non-Aryan' blood had deeply shocked his widowed father, and that he felt that he, an only son, could not go against his father's convictions. Therefore all that had been between us must remain just a happy memory.

I was heart-broken and firmly vowed never to fall in love again. One hurt was enough. I believe my mother, too, suffered though she never once referred to the matter when it was all over.

More and more, politics entered daily life, embittering many a personal relationship.

In spite of the reconciliation politics of Briand and Stresemann, France's and Germany's Foreign Ministers, in spite of the evacuation of the Ruhr in 1924, and the consequent acceptance of Germany into the League of Nations, the people of the Weimar Republic were deeply divided, dissatisfied with conditions under a prosperous enough surface. The selection of members of the Communist and National-Socialist parties to the *Reichstag*, with the loss of democratic seats, was a clear indication of growing unrest.

It all happened in a country which had not yet understood the meaning of democracy, with dozens of political parties splitting the vote, and making for constant changes in government and all-round instability. Eventually the crash of the New York money market brought in its wake unemployment, waves of strikes, depression and misery. All the time voices demanding a new leadership grew louder and louder. An articulate minority still sought a cure for excessive nationalism in notions of a United Europe, the *Pan Europa*, propagated by Count Coudenhove-Kalerghi. A cultural and economic union was to be followed eventually by a political one.

My mother had absorbed Father's enthusiasms for a united Europe, and in the late twenties used all my holidays and the little money we could spare to give me what she called a 'European education', an education I had missed getting through the more conventional academic channels. I was to visit Belgium, France, Austria, parts of Italy and Yugoslavia. Wherever I was taken I saw people trying to live with the past and at the time settling into an uneasy peace. War had been over for almost a decade.

My travels began one fine summer's day in the main railway station at Brussels. I stood flabbergasted watching the traffic and the crowds, when a good-humoured but firm rebuke came from Mother. 'Don't stand there looking stupid, say something. You've learnt French, haven't you?' She was goading me into being at ease in a foreign country and speaking a foreign tongue. Her words had the desired effect. In my halting schoolgirl French I made a porter take our luggage to a cab for the Hotel Métropole in the Place Brouckère where we had booked a room. Luggage then was pretty formidable. With drip-dry garments not yet invented, everything had to be taken at least in triplicate in case laundering was not available en route. Hats, a necessity, especially in the city, were carried in separate hat boxes. However, we did not follow the current fashion of sending large trunks in advance. Mother believed in travelling as light as possible, a habit I have since developed into a fine art.

The Hotel Métropole was my first introduction to, what at least to me, was 'the big world'. It was elegant in an Edwardian way, with impeccable service. I happily tiptoed along its deep-carpeted corridors. Brussels' broad boulevards and tree-lined avenues impressed me, and I returned again and again to the Grand Place to look at the handsome medieval houses. There were museums and picture galleries to be admired and, of course, the shops. Mother had secretly hoarded a little money to buy me my first proper evening dress. It was of a pale pink crêpe-de-chine, sequin-embroidered, and soon to be put to good use. Shopkeepers were friendly and helpful. Forbearing with our anything but fluent French, they were pleased to see us make the effort.

The atmosphere was very different when after a few days we moved to the Belgian coast. There the population had not forgotten the events of barely twelve years ago when the German armies had poured into their peaceful country. The underlying feeling of hostility found expression in graffiti stating quite clearly: '*A bas les boches*' and posters in some shops, hotels and boarding houses saying that Germans were not welcome. There were even some anti-*boches* slogans on small paper flags flying over sand castles on the beach. The mostly Flemish-speaking locals behaved with dignity but kept German tourists at a safe distance. Through the recommendation of a Belgian friend Mother and I were fortunate in finding a small *taverne*, run by the owners who were two lively people with a great sense of fun. They took a philosophic view of the past, and generously and cheerfully entertained their small company of international guests. The food was excellent and plentiful in the true Flemish tradition. Luckily there was also plenty of exercise. Fine sandy beaches invited bathing, ball games and 'eurythmics', the fashionable rhythmic movements, aimed at producing the 'body beautiful'. *Le Joyeux Troubadour*, an elderly man, earning a humble living by playing the guitar, was always willing to provide the music for our capers.

At night we all assembled in the basement of our pub, *Le Cave*, where I learnt the Charleston, and the pink, sequined dress was just right. Also, for the first time since my broken romance I enjoyed the company of young men. I had adopted a very cynical attitude, not wanting to suffer again. My heart had once been broken, and now I set out to give it away in bits. It proved pleasant enough. We chatted, we danced and with Mamma's consent, of course, I accepted invitations to be rowed along the network of canals which spread out into the hinterland of the Belgian coast. At some picturesque farmhouse inn we would tie up our boat and have *café cramique*, strong coffee with a thickly buttered slice of currant loaf. A young Englishman who had stayed behind in Cologne after the war, to become of all things, an agent for Scottish tweeds there, took me to a smart cocktail bar, *L'heure Bleue*. I tried my English on him and received what, I am sure, were very exaggerated compliments.

There was no generation gap at our dancing evenings. While we enjoyed ourselves to the music of a three-man jazz band, older members of the party sat at clean-scrubbed wooden tables, with a carafe of red or white wine, humming the latest tunes. 'Valencia' was our great favourite, played with much frantic noise from the saxophone. These evening gatherings had some of the high spirits of a *kermesse*, a Flemish fair, due certainly to our genial hosts. At midnight *le patron* would clap his hands to the rhythm of the jazz, and begin serving sour herring and *tartines*, small sandwiches with cold meats or *crevettes* fresh from the sea. There might also be a hot steaming fish soup. This copious 'snack' was the signal for the party to end and everybody was expected to retire to their respective rooms.

Two weeks went in a flash, and it was time to go home. On our way we paid a visit to Bruges, with its beautiful old buildings and canals. It seemed to be of another time or century. At the *beguinage* we bought some lace, just as it came off the lace-pillow of one of the old women, sitting working in the sunshine. The following winter I put it round fine lawn mats. One of them has survived and is still used on my cheeseboard. During a short stop at Cologne I saw the Rhine for the first time, that river which to the Germans has an almost mystical meaning. I enjoyed the fine scenery, the cheerfulness of the people and Cologne's beautiful cathedral. At a restaurant in the hills high above the river we ate salmon caught that morning. I fear salmon has long since disappeared from the Rhine. It was at one time a sought-after delicacy.

Home again, workaday life went on as usual until the following year mother planned a journey to Paris. I was very excited at the thought of coming face to face with this fabled city. In France, strangely enough, we did not come across the slightest sign of resentment of the 'arch enemy'. On the contrary everyone gave very good service and was anxious to please. When in a restaurant in the Bois de Boulogne my mother looked round vaguely on having *Raie au Beurre noire* served with just a hunk of bread, the waiter smiled and said: 'Pardon Madame, I forgot completely that our neighbours from across the Rhine like potatoes with their fish. I'll get some at once.' And he did.

During a sightseeing visit to Versailles the guide explained the many historical paintings of famous battles France had won through the centuries. And lightheartedly turning towards the German tourists in the party, he added: 'the ones she has lost may be seen *à Berlin.*' The image of Germany, the traditional enemy, definitely seemed to be fading in France. There was faith in the 'Europeanness' of the Weimar Republic. In the sunshine of early summer Paris showed its proverbial 'gay' side. The pavement cafés were crowded, and we sat for hours over a cup of coffee and a glass of brown rum, watching the passers-by. Montmartre still had the quality of a village, and Bohemian types really lived there, and were not just stage-managed for the tourists. At the *bouquinistes* along the Seine a fine eighteenth-century copperplate or a coloured lithographed view of the city could be bought for a pound or less. One of the highlights of our trip was seeing Mistinguette, all clad in pink ostrich feathers give a spirited performance in *Ça c'est Paris*. The music for its most catching numbers went back with me in my suitcase, to be hammered out on the piano for months to come.

Our next holiday was spent in Vienna and beyond. My mother had known the city in its imperial splendour, and to her nothing was quite the same. As for myself I marvelled in the new experience, taking in the wonderful sights. For the first time I had a little money to do some shopping of my own. I returned from the Ring, the Graben or the Kärntnerstrasse, Vienna's elegant shopping streets, with an embroidered sweater in the then very fashionable lime coloured soft wool and my first ever beach suit, consisting of slacks and a Chinese type of jacket in pale blue linen. I was very proud of my possessions. At the city's famous hotel we consumed *Sachertorte* with *Schlagobers*, luscious whipped cream, and drank endless cups of strong coffee – said to have been brought to Vienna by the Turks – in the many cafés and pastry shops. I went back again and again to the Spanish Riding School where the Lippizaner horses performed superbly. We attended the performance of a play by the Austrian poet and dramatist, Franz Grillparzer, at the *Burgtheater* and in the scented air of a moonlit park listened to waltzes, the conductor playing the fiddle in the true Viennese manner. We went to the Prater, the city's great park, when the chestnuts were in flower, and on the very day when boys and girls after their First Communion are taken out by their godmothers for their time-honoured treat. Straight from St. Stephen's great cathedral they came driving in a *Fiaker*, a smart horse-drawn carriage, to be entertained to hot chocolate and cake. A ride on the Great Wheel finished our day.

However, not all was charm and springtime in Vienna. Many who at one time had known 'the sweet life' now continued at mere existence level, some even in dire poverty. We were introduced to the widow of a once famous actor who had now to rely on charity and the help of younger and more fortunate friends to pay her bills for light, heating and the most basic food. Even then she left her two-room flatlet each day to find warmth and shelter in art galleries and libraries. These visits also provided her with the only mental nourishment now within her reach. Together with many of her contemporaries she ate many a meal in public soup kitchens. Though inflation in Austria had not been as drastic as in Germany, fortunes had melted away, and the elderly found it hard to cope in a completely changed social structure.

We continued the journey by bus through the Dolomites. On the height of the Pordoi Pass where much fighting had taken place, we stopped to pay homage to the dead of the Great War. Bunches of wild flowers were placed under the wooden crosses of Austrian and Italian soldiers alike. I put a glowing-red *Alpenrose*, picked nearby, on the grave of a young Italian, and remembered my father's verdict on the horror and futility of all wars. Our immediate destination was Bozen. Though now belonging to Italy and officially called Bolzano, the lovely old town had a completely un-Latin, Austrian, even southern German atmosphere. At that time there was much agitation for a return of the Southern Tyrol to Germany after the 1921 plebiscite had been vetoed by the Entente.

We took rooms at the old established *Hotel Zum Greifen*, where meals were served in the open at street level. Guests were sheltered from the crowds by screens of ivy growing in wooden boxes. However, this barrier broke down every time youngsters began singing patriotic songs in the streets. Hotel guests got up, hands were linked as emotion grew and shouts of 'Remember Andreas Hofer' were heard. The *Sandwirt*, Andreas Hofer, who fought and died for freedom under the Napoleonic yoke, was a living folk memory. It usually took two indulgent smiling *carabinieri* to turn up on the horizon, smartly walking in the direction of the hotel, for the singing and fraternizing to stop.

Travel in Austria had made my mother wish for us to see more of the former Hapsburg Empire, and in 1929, long before Yugoslavia became a tourist's paradise, we boarded a small coaster at Trieste to sail down the Dalmatian coast. Our plans had caused much head-shaking among older relatives. Two women alone in a Balkan country: what would the accommodation be like, and the food? We were undeterred, and the adventure, as it was called, proved well worth it. The Adriatic was at its calm best, and a warm sun shone from a cloudless sky. We stopped at the quiet and dream-like islands of Hvar and Corcula, to dock eventually at Split, still often referred to by its Italian name, Spalato.

In this grand port people had not yet found their true identity. Countryside and architecture combined to give a completely Italian impression, the people were obviously Slav; yet the heritage of the Austrian Empire lingered. My mother, not knowing any Balkan language, called a taxi driver in her best Italian. He answered in a very Austrian-sounding German, saying that he was very glad and proud to speak her native language. Life in the old Empire, he added nostalgically, was wonderful.

As we settled for a week in a small hotel inside the ruins of Diocletian's great palace, and built of the very stones, we began to explore Split's treasures and her shopping opportunities. Silk then was a great bargain; a couple of shillings would buy a metre. We were naturally very interested, and began haunting the many silk mercers' shops. Eventually we decided on the one we liked best. A tall, brown-skinned man received us with great courtesy. We chose silks for several dresses, our negotiations conducted in faultless German. We had been told about the chance to have the material made up on the spot. And sure enough, we were taken to the backshop where the proprietor's wife sat at a sewing machine, making up garments cheaply and at short notice. To our astonishment, we saw shelves draped in the colours of the Hapsburg monarchy and a bust of the Emperor Franz Josef. Noticing our surprise, the master of the house lifted some drapes, and behind them were hidden several brass instruments. The mercer then explained that he had been a band master in an Austrian regiment, and this was his sanctum. He then looked out of the window, and having reassured himself that nobody was watching or listening, he put a record on an old-fashioned gramaphone. Then our measurements were taken to the muffled sound of the Radetzky-March. *Sic transit gloria mundi*.

Dubrovnik-Ragusa, where we spent our second week at the pretty Imperial Hotel, still retained a very Austrian atmosphere. Crowds of young naval officers, clad in immaculate white uniforms, came to the hotel every night to dance Viennese waltzes in the open, vine-clad courtyard under a starlit sky. They kissed hands after every dance, a most romantic experience for the young women at the receiving end. The walled city of Dubrovnik itself was also romantic with a mixture of striking buildings of many styles and periods, testifying to the once free and independent republic. Oleander flowered by the roadside and olives, umbrella pines and agaves stood high above the cliffs against a deep blue sky. Tall handsome peasants in colourful costume came into the town to exchange their produce for silver-buttoned waistcoats, bags woven of vegetable-dyed wool, soft hand-made shoes and bright rugs.

For a couple of years we continued to explore bits of Europe at twelve-monthly intervals. We saw great stretches of Germany. The peasant-baroque churches of Bavaria with their light-hearted grace became my favourites. We visited the medieval towns on the Romantic Road which leads south from Franconia, and tasted Rhine and Moselle vintages in the spots where they are grown. We spent two memorable weeks in a large hotel on Lake Constance, memorable for the fact that I tried out surfing there although I spent more time in the water of Lake Constance than on it.

The stay was memorable, too, for an event which was to disturb my mind often in later years. On our first night at dinner we were asked by the head waiter if we minded having another guest at our table. When we agreed there appeared a very well preserved elderly man who turned out to be a Swiss industrialist, widely travelled and interesting to talk to. I noticed that whenever I was out swimming, playing tennis or in some way joining company of my own age, the gentleman sought out my mother. Sometimes the three of us enjoyed tea together on the sunny hotel terrace overlooking a wide stretch of the lake. Then one evening my mother came laughing into the room we shared, telling me she had just had a proposal of marriage. The Swiss gentleman, widowed for some years, had asked her to be his companion for the rest of his life. He had also said that he liked me and would gladly send me to university if I cared to take up a career which I had longed for not so many years ago.

I reacted hysterically. Never could I see any man in my greatly loved father's place, and I cried all that night. Greatly disturbed, my mother reassured me, saying that she had not taken the whole thing seriously and certainly would never take a single step without my full and heartfelt agreement. The gentleman departed the next day, and he was never mentioned again between Mother and myself. However, in the future and when things were to happen as they did, I often thought of my behaviour as neurotic and selfish, believing that a Swiss marriage might have spared my mother much suffering and sorrow and might well have prolonged her life.

Again and again we went to Holland which through my father's kin was not a foreign country to us. Land reclamation on the Zuidersee had only just begun, and we sailed to many a remote fishing village where people still wore costume as their daily dress and only changed their wooden clogs for shoes on Sundays. We saw red round cheeses piled high in the market at Edam.

At home, great changes were to take place. As a result of worsening economic conditions my boss decided to sell part of his enterprise. In the autumn of 1931 'my' bookshop changed hands. I was not happy and resigned.

I had for some time contemplated opening a small bookshop of my own, and encouraged by customers and friends I plunged in at the deep end. There were, too, warnings from well-meaning friends, pointing to the political clouds gathering on the horizon. I fear that politically I was naive, and I did not listen. I just could not imagine our young and much treasured democracy disappearing in a maelstrom of terror. Premises were found, I borrowed money from my long-suffering mamma, and with the assistance of a fellow bookseller our up-to-date little shop opened in the spring of 1932.

There were well-wishers galore, telegrams and a sea of flowers. On the opening night we were kept busy till well after dark when we sat down with a few close friends over a bottle of champagne. I was prepared to work hard, make small demands, and establish myself over the years. I had loved what I had seen of Europe but I also loved my home and had a sense of continuity, settling where my father's family had lived for generations. Long holidays were out for the time being, but late in January 1933 Mother and I escaped for a few days to the snow and sun of the Harz mountains. We enjoyed long walks where the big pine trees cast blue shadows in the clear light. I did short stints on the nursery slopes, and managed my skis well enough to join a *langlauf* excursion, returning to the hotel at dusk, glowing and happy. Everyday life and particularly politics seemed far away. On our last day Mother and I went for a long walk, stopping to take our packed lunch at a remote ski hut, full of cheerful, noisy hikers and skiers. There was a sudden hush when the radio announced that Adolf Hitler had been made Chancellor.

Germany's slide into barbarism had begun. A heavy cloud hung over the journey home.

PART III
The Advent of Nazism

Chapter 8

On the 1st February 1933 we returned from the deceiving brightness of the Harz mountains to a town wrapped in chilly gloom. The air was heavy with damp, skies were grey, and people's faces drawn and apprehensive. The usual small-town gossips were silent. Nobody wanted to be caught expressing an opinion.

The sudden news of President Hindenburg having called in Hitler to take over the office of Chancellor had confirmed to many how desperate the political and economic situation really was. There was fear about, fear of the unknown, fear of danger, fear that the politically apathetic German middle class had been too little alert for too long. As militant Brownshirts marched in the streets, sporting huge swastika flags and singing the *Horst Wessel* song, many wished that they had taken the pronouncements of *Mein Kampf* more seriously. 'Heads will roll in the sand', 'Jews out', 'Jewish pigs are our Misfortune', and similar graffiti appeared on walls and scaffoldings. Tension increased as nobody knew what would happen next.

In our town, typical of a German community of some 20,000 inhabitants, the National Socialist Party had increasingly attracted members for many and different reasons. There were those who sincerely and honestly believed that Germany needed a change of direction, and that a new leadership would end unemployment and depression. Others had never been able to come to terms with defeat on the battlefields and the Treaty of Versailles that followed: they rallied hopefully to a patriotic cause.

There were also the failures, the unsuccessful who hoped for promotion, for help from the party, even for personal gain. There were a good few ruffians and criminal elements, but to begin with anti-semitism, though evident in all Nazi teachings, did not over-assert itself.

The small Jewish community of our town had for centuries lived in harmony with its fellow citizens, completely identifying with and accepted by them. Nobody thought that this state could ever change.

Meantime life in the bookshop went on much as usual, although instinctively people spoke in whispers when discussing the present state of affairs. Tension was in the air.

I felt desperately unhappy, not just because of my own personal background but because of the general impact a complete Nazi takeover would have on the Germany which I considered my home. My whole way of life, the cosmopolitanism and pacifism which I had been brought up to believe in, was savagely threatened. The ground beneath my feet was shaking.

In mid-February the annual dance of the Riding Club was to take place. It was an event I looked forward to normally, but I decided not to attend this time. It was no good embarrassing anybody by my presence, and I feared that I might well be tempted to express views which might provoke anger in some, and would certainly be considered dangerous to hold. As soon as it became known that I had not bought a ticket, members of the Club called at the bookshop and at my home, wondering what was wrong. They hoped, they said, it was not politics which had prompted my declining to go to the dance.

'You don't pay any attention to that madman,' one of my visitors remarked casually. 'Bet you, his time is almost up; he won't last much longer.'

The *Deutschnationalen* was a party many club members belonged to; they thought they knew it all. 'Give Hitler just enough rope to hang himself. That's just what is being done. The Nazis are done for anyway.'

This was in February 1933.

In the end persuasion worked. I gave in, went to the ball and enjoyed myself. Up to a point, that is. Everybody was as nice as ever, and some went out of their way to be even nicer. That I did not like as I had never felt myself to be different, and I did not want special treatment now. On the other hand, I became almost convinced that night that things might unexpectedly change for the better. I felt a certain euphoria and I danced into the early hours.

It was not to last.

On the night of 27th February the Berlin *Reichstag* went on fire. Dread of Communism, always present, reached hysterical heights, and rumours of a Communist plot provided the Nazis with a welcome pretext for emergency measures. All civil liberties were suspended, and the police given absolute powers. Uniformed Nazi stormtroopers were seconded as *Hilfspolizei* – auxiliary police – and by a stroke of the pen the party became the country's dominant security force.

Communists and Social Democrats were called Marxist criminals, and houses of suspects were raided day and night for weapons, anti-Nazi literature or leaflets presumed to be intended to bring a counter-revolution through Communist infiltration. One or two highly respected citizens went into hiding or even fled the country. There were rumours of suicides, some committed, it was whispered, at pistol point. The bookshop had become very quiet. People attended to their business hurriedly without the few moments of friendly gossip or even five minutes of literary small talk. An air of leaden uneasiness hung over the place.

Elections to the *Reichstag* were to be held on 5th March, and Nazi propaganda became more aggressive as Hitler's voice boomed over the loudspeakers at every street corner. There were daily torchlight processions with much shouting of *Sieg Heil* where brutal violence soon silenced even the weakest opposition. All the same, the National Socialist Party only gained support from half the electorate, but at the end of May a law stabilizing February's emergency measures and giving the Government absolute powers was to be passed by the *Reichstag* against passionate opposition by the Social Democrats. Totalitarianism and dictatorship were closing in on Germany.

Local elections took place on 12th March without changing the position much. Masses now jumped on to the party band-wagon, motivated by fear or the wish to get on. Friends and acquaintances, even the ones that had so ardently desired my presence at the dance, only some three weeks earlier, now deliberately crossed the street or stopped under a shop window so as not to be forced into speaking to me in passing. Many former well-wishers avoided the bookshop not wishing to risk careless talk.

Voices of dissent were now almost silenced as papers were banned, and some of their editors shot while 'trying to escape from protective custody'. In our small town beatings-up of known protestors were a daily occurrence as were arrests and imprisonment without trial. The dreaded word 'concentration camp' was always present, and the name of Dachau, once an artists's colony, became a horrifying threat. Civil servants and employees, not trusted, were dismissed, and often thugs and jailbirds, having become useful, took their place. Terror ruled under an apparently normal surface, and the slightest criticism became dangerous as willing informers lurked round every corner. Nobody could be depended on any longer, as more and more joined the party simply to protect themselves, their jobs and their families. Civil courage had become the first casualty and acquiescence was the rule of the day. The National Socialists, with all other parties obliterated, now were the state.

Press, radio, the arts, education in schools and universities came under the party's control, and the obnoxious word *Gleichschaltung* – bringing into line with Nazi doctrine – was on everybody's lips.

Late in March a national ceremony in Potsdam's Garrison Church, staged by Hitler and Hindenburg, declared the beginning of a new epoch in German history. It certainly was, and a shameful one.

Democracy, young only in Germany, was dead before it was ever given a chance to establish itself fully.

In April, Hitler felt strong enough to make the first step in 'solving the Jewish question'. Shops and business enterprises owned by Jews were to be boycotted on 1st April. Jews were to be cut off from their fellow citizens, set apart to be easily recognised. The excuse put forward, if indeed excuse was needed, was the tale that international Jewry was spreading abroad lies about persecution and cruelties in order to discredit the new Germany. The boycott was to last until the Jewish campaign against the regime had ceased.

As I arrived in the bookshop on a fine spring morning I found two enormous stormtroopers posted outside. The men did not touch me. They did not even look at me, but slogans were smeared all over the windows and customers were kept from entering the shop. There was some shuffling and arguing but no serious incident.

It is difficult after these many years to describe my feelings. They were a mixture of contempt, of rebellion and of instant determination to leave Germany. I knew for certain that I could never live, work and be content again in a country where freedom was abolished, and the rule of might was now right.

That morning I telephoned a lawyer, asked for the proper proceedings, and on that very day applied to have my name eliminated officially from the firm's ownership. That done, I went home to cry as the whole misery of the situation dawned on me. Naturally, my mother was very distressed.

My experience had been so violent that I had not even stopped to discuss matters with her before making a decision. Childhood and family friends risked their own future to come and speak to me, asking me to think again, implying that I had rushed things quite unnecessarily. They called my action precipitous, some frivolous or even cowardly. A much-loved uncle shouted to me over the telephone. I remained firm, and my mother stood by me.

When they burnt 'un-German' books in May of that year, I went back to the bookshop secretly, and saved some of my favourites. Smuggled out of Germany later, they still have a treasured place on my shelves.

With little or no help from outside, a long period of feeling like a mouse in a trap lay ahead of me. Mother, loyal as always, suffered in silence, never even mentioning with a single word the financial loss which was practically all hers.

The months following the spring of 1933 affected my life very deeply. Until then I had been a member of a small, closely-knit community where everybody knew everybody else, and took a friendly interest in a neighbour's joys and sorrows. All that changed overnight. Anyone whose 'race', religion or ancestry was not one hundred per cent 'Aryan' became suddenly isolated and ostracised, excluded from all normal activities. Fortunately my mother and I were like good friends, drawn very close together by my father's early death. Now, more than ever, did we depend on each other. We only left the house together, and even then we did so reluctantly. Often the town was beflagged on the pretext of some national holiday, and hundreds of swastikas swung overhead. In shops we were served hurriedly, almost furtively, as people were afraid that by paying attention and encouraging us to linger, they might be tempted to speak their mind. Many would have liked to talk freely, but terror completely silenced them. After Dachau, Oranienburg and Sachsenhausen became dreaded names as concentration camps proliferated. Fear of the newly established secret police – the *Gestapo* – ruled supreme. Your one-time close friend or neighbour might have joined its ranks.

Gleichschaltung had now brought all intellectual activity in line with the system. So we had no wish to attend theatres or concerts. The radio, controlled by the Minister of Propaganda, Joseph Goebbels, pouring out a stream of abuse for the old, and rules for the new, Germany, supplied no relief. Papers and journals toed the party line. We still had our books, but somehow reading seemed irrelevant. In fact, it was hard to concentrate on anything but one thought: How do I get away from a nightmare? Plans for emigration occupied our days and much of our nights. Sleep had become fitful and nights frightening for two women alone in a big house. A heavy footstep at dusk or dawn could well be that of a jack-booted jailer.

We wrote to many embassies and obtained piles of informative material. One day we would become planters in some distant part of Africa, next day saw us nursing in the Far East or looking after a wealthy sultan's children. I even fancied becoming a mounted policewoman when I heard that traffic policemen or women able to handle horses were in short supply in some parts of the world.

The sober reality was quite different from these therapeutic pipe-dreams. Most countries gave permanent work permits only to a few among the distinguished in science and the arts, and all emigration needed money. Early on the Nazi government had blocked accounts, and strict rules were laid down for money transfers. Exit permits were required for going abroad, even temporarily. When our thoughts turned to discussing matters with our Dutch relations, we applied for permits, but were refused over and over again. Then in July 1933, Hitler concluded a Concordat with the Vatican, and thereby appeased many silently-doubting Catholics and even the more gullible among the bourgeois intelligentsia. More safely in the saddle, the government could afford a slight relaxation of security. Unexpectedly my mother and I received exit visas for a short stay in Holland.

The journey turned out to be a disappointment.

Though it was wonderful to leave – even if only for a few weeks – a country which to us had become claustrophobic and a prison, realities on the other side of the frontier were disillusioning. In Holland nobody quite believed in the necessity for us to emigrate. My decision to resign from the bookselling business in April of that year was still considered hasty, indeed hysterical. Nazi propaganda had deluded public opinion outside Germany too. If not a glorious hero, Hitler was at least thought of as a man who would 'settle' in time, having perhaps saved Germany from the extremes of the Left. Anti-semitism was played down, and excesses blamed on individuals, acting impulsively and surely without the knowledge of the *Führer*. It was maddening for us to hear that sort of thing over and over again. Not a soul in the solid comfort of a small Dutch town would or could grasp the truth and the meaning of the evil threat of

Nazism. We left disheartened, almost angry.

A wearisome and desperate autumn and winter followed, with all attempts at solving our problem thwarted in some way or other. It was all made worse for me who had worked for years and become independent, to be forced to rely completely on my mother. After the debacle of the inflation she had only slowly and painstakingly built up reserves again through letting parts of our property as shops and offices, and carefully investing restituted money in the new and safer currency. Big inroads were now made into these small savings. Then suddenly one morning there arrived a letter from people we had met while travelling some years ago. We had since exchanged Christmas cards and the odd letter. But this was different. After giving some personal news they asked in a casual manner whether I would care to visit them in the spring, and see a little of Scotland. In fact, the family lived not far from Edinburgh. Something in the tone of the letter, something between the lines, revealed an understanding of our situation nobody had shown before. Delighted with the first good thing that had come my way for a long time, and encouraged by my mother, I accepted the invitation, and started making preparations for the journey. Evenings were now spent in reading aloud H.V. Morton's *In Search of Scotland.* There was much we did not understand, yet we learnt a great deal about a country which until then had been to us a land of grey mists, of white ladies haunting ancient castles, and hearts yearning forever for the Highlands.

By 1934 it was the government's policy to let 'undesirable' citizens leave Germany for a while 'in order to explore emigration possibilities'. Even though there was no immediate prospect, I gave this reason when making application for an exit permit.

It was granted almost at once.

Chapter 9

Early in May I left my mother, not without qualms, but believing that our short separation might bring hope for the future. I stopped for some ten days in London with the family of a schoolfriend of my father's. In the eighteen-nineties, as a young boy, this man had been sent from Germany to receive a business training in the City, then thought of as the financial centre of the world. He had married the boss's daughter, and had to all intents and purposes become an Englishman, going to his city office every morning complete with bowler hat and rolled umbrella. The family pampered and spoiled me and took me the rounds of London. In spite of my halting English, in spite of the vastness of the city and its many bewildering aspects, I did not feel a stranger. There was air to breathe in, and I laughed more than I had done for many a long month. Politically in London also the people did not comprehend the real state of affairs in Germany. Hardly anyone thought of Hitler as a menace to the whole concept of humanity, and, as far as I could make out, quite a few discovered some praiseworthy aims in the new regime. Even my father's friend who knew more about Germany than most of his fellow countrymen shrugged the matter off as a passing phase, not worth worrying about too much. Nobody seemed to comprehend what was really happening inside Germany.

The time came for my trip to Scotland, and I decided to go by bus to see as much as I could of the countryside. It was also cheaper than going by train. To my regret there were no day buses available, but I passed Marble Arch on a beautiful May evening to get on to the Great North Road for the first time in my life. Somewhere en route I had my first fish-and-chips supper, and afterwards went to sleep in the most comfortable bus seat I had ever known. A friendly driver wished us 'goodnight' and switched off the lights inside the bus. When I woke it was morning and somebody said: 'We are in Scotland now.' Sure enough, we soon stopped at Greenlaw and had a good breakfast in a little café close to a neo-classical building which I admired.

Not long after, we reached Edinburgh where my host was to meet me at the Mound. I was struck by the beauty of the Castle and the whole scene against a bright morning sky. I did not then realise that it was the beginning of a relationship which was to last a lifetime. Though I had only met the quiet, gentle Scotsman who now welcomed me for a short time on our travels in Holland, I was delighted to see him again. During our short walk to the bus, he exuded a warmth and kindness, most comforting to me. He showed more perception of my situation than anybody had done so far. We were soon on our way to a cottage not far from Dalkeith where his family, wife, teenage daughter and small son, greeted me with affection. Their home was one in a row of small bungalows and the prettiness of the gardens struck me at once. They were charming and in sharp contrast to the surrounding mining villages which I was to find dreary.

My honeymoon with Scotland was, as perhaps are all honeymoons, a mixture of bliss and the need to adapt to a new love. It was wonderful to wake every morning and realise that there were no stormtroopers in the streets, no shouting, no swastikas and no need for wondering what the next hour might bring. From my host's home within easy reach of Edinburgh we went frequently on sightseeing excursions. As a special treat I was taken on a bus tour to the Trossachs and had my first glimpse of Stirling Castle and the Highlands. That day stands out in my memory because I suddenly knew to what extent I had to adapt myself anywhere away from my old background. It was what in Germany is called the second day of Whitsun, and I was amazed to see work going on everywhere, and no sign of festiveness. I was told rather sternly that it was 'popish' to celebrate these holy days excessively. I could then not prevent a pang of what may have been homesickness, a nostalgic thought of outings in sunny woods, with everybody dressed up, and festive meals of early strawberries, spring chicken and tender salads, even in time of austerity; all ingredients of a Continental Whitsun.

The most wonderful joy, however, was that everybody, without exception, was so very kind to me, completely overlooking my shortcomings in the use of English and my awkwardness in dealing with new situations. The Scots, at least the ones I met, completely belied the myth of the stand-offish British.

In spite of my disheartening experiences since the advent of the Nazis and in spite of all my madcap plans of emigrating to the far ends of the earth and changing my work altogether, I was deep down still very keen on working with books.

So one day I picked up courage and asked my host, who was a civil servant, whether he knew any booksellers in Edinburgh as I should much like to meet one. This sprang partly from the wish to exchange experiences with a colleague in another country but behind it lurked, almost subconsciously, the hope of perhaps finding a way out of Germany. My host immediately got in touch with John Menzies, the wholesale booksellers. He knew one of their directors. This man, a Mr. Fraser, was happy to see me. I remember now meeting him in his small office in their Rose Street buildings in Edinburgh. He was extremely nice and after we had exchanged some pleasantries he explained laughingly that a book warehouse like Menzies' was as dull in Edinburgh as it was in Leipzig. However, he would introduce me to what he called 'the leading bookseller not just of Edinburgh but perhaps of Scotland'. In no time he had made an appointment with Mr. Ainslie Thin, the University Bookseller, and he took me personally to the impressive shop opposite the University. There I was received with great courtesy and soon Ainslie Thin and his brother Tom, also in the business, and I were involved in a longish talk among 'experts'. At the end of it the two men proposed that during the few remaining weeks of my holiday I might like to come in as often as I wished and enjoy the freedom of their shop to see how things were done in Scotland. I was delighted with the prospect and hurried back to tell my hosts of my good fortune. I had found the bookshop bigger and more interesting than any I had ever seen and the owners had impressed me as excellent representatives of their old and honoured trade.

For the rest of my stay I went to Thin's every day. I inspected all the departments, looked at their stock and order system, at cataloguing and general administration. I was even daring enough to make some suggestions and explain how I was used to handling certain matters differently.

During my last few days in Scotland, I sat one morning high on a pair of steps in Thin's second-hand basement. I was looking at some interesting old books when I was startled by the appearance of Ainslie Thin. Gesturing me not to come down the steps but to continue my inspection, he assured me that he had only a few words to say. Without further ado he went on to tell me that after consultation with his brother and others in the firm, he would like to offer me a position. The Foreign Department had never quite recovered after the First World War and perhaps I might be able to build it up and look after it in general. There was a snag. The Ministry of Labour did not grant working permits to foreigners unless they were doing work no British subject could do. However, he had a suggestion to make. Would I be able and prepared to come for an unpaid trainee year which, of course, he knew to be that only as far as language and changed circumstances were concerned. Yet, such a year might provide the chance for proving that I was, in fact, doing special work.

'There is no need to say anything just now,' he continued, 'just think it all over.'

And with that he was gone.

He left me dumbfounded on the top of my ladder. My head was in a whirl. Here I was being offered a job, just the kind of job I would pick in an ideal world. There was a way out of Germany but . . . how could I live without money? How would my mother fare in an increasingly hostile country? Though the Nazi regime wanted to get rid of Jews, there was no way of transferring money abroad. We were actually completely trapped if not given an opportunity to earn a living abroad.

I felt totally confused when I left Scotland. The Germany I returned to was on the brink of more horror.

On 30th June 1934 in Upper Bavaria, Captain Ernst Röhm, chief of the S.A. and Hitler's former close friend, was shot out of hand with many others, most of them high-ranking personalities in the party. Politicians, writers and citizens of all kinds who had incurred the *Führer*'s displeasure were murdered all over Germany. Among them was General Kurt von Schleicher, Former Chancellor of the *Reich* and his wife. The excuse for the purge was alleged offences of individuals, and the rumoured existence of a plot against the Third Reich. On 25 July of that year the Austrian Chancellor Dollfuss was killed in a Nazi-inspired coup. Soon after Hindenburg, by that time an ineffective old man, died in retirement on his Prussian estate. Hitler now proclaimed himself *Führer* and Chancellor. This new show of strength further frightened many thousands into submission. People became even more careful in what they said and did. The Great Powers were neither willing nor able to intervene in the internal affairs of a sovereign state, and an overthrow of Hitler became less likely as each day passed.

In this atmosphere my mother, in her always determined and equally unselfish way, announced one morning that she had made arrangements with relations abroad to send me a small sum of money every month, in order that I could live in Scotland for a year. She knew, she said, that this must be done, as it was an opportunity which might in time mean a way out for us both. What is more, she also had enough money available to accompany me to Scotland, stay for a month or two, and see me settled.

There was no contradicting my mother once she had made up her mind, and late in September we arrived in Edinburgh. We had not booked rooms as Mother was determined to see me established in a good boarding house and stay with me there for a little so that she knew and could picture my new, immediate surroundings.

In Waverley Station, in her best schoolgirl English my mother made this clear to a tall, very friendly bobby. He looked at me and said, 'Surely a student, isn't she? They all stay in Marchmont.' He then directed us to a number six tram and told us to get off 'at the top of Marchmont'. There would be a dairy there and they always had a list of vacancies. We thanked him and followed his advice. Sure enough, there was a dairy 'at the top of Marchmont' with the promised list of vacancies. They immediately directed us to a boarding house close by, adding that they were certain we would find it satisfactory.

We did and got a room at the back of the house with a beautiful view of the Blackford Hills. Mother made sure that I would keep this room after her departure. She was so anxious that she should see me settled in a reasonable place of some comfort. In the days to follow she discovered Woolworth and there bought me a little crockery and some knives and forks, in case I might be tempted to eat fruit or anything extra I would bring in, just out of paper bags. That would have been squalor to her. She strongly advised me to eat some fruit each day as she found the Scottish diet lacking in fresh fruit and vegetables.

My trainee permit had been secured, and all was well, particularly as my mother greatly enjoyed the relief from daily anxiety. Again we were shown much friendship. Lots of people volunteered to show Mother the sights of Edinburgh while I was at work. We were taken out to lunches and dinners, and saw our first plays in English performed on the Lyceum stage. Even though we could not follow every word, those evenings were a great treat to us. And more than anything else we were aware of the feeling of freedom and deeply grateful for it. We had our first experience of a genuine Scottish High Tea where we saw with amazement a huge home-baked steak and kidney pie served. All we knew of 'English tea' was the then fashionable 'Five o'clock' with dainty pieces of fruit cake and cups of strong tea, taken with milk.

Alas, the thought that my mother's money was running out and that in a certain number of weeks she would have to go back to Germany, was always with us. It lay like a dark shadow over everything we were doing. At last the dreaded moment arrived. Early one November morning in drizzling rain and general misery we said goodbye at Waverley Station. I made my way back to Thin's, alone and depressed.

In the weeks and months to follow letters from my mother showed that all was not well. In the spring of 1935 therefore, I felt that I had to visit her. A trainee permit allowed me to move freely to and from Germany, and a good friend helped me secure a few pupils for German conversation, whose 'gifts' solved the problem of finding money for the journey. I travelled on the old *Grangemouth* of the Gibson-Rankin line from Leith to Antwerp for under ten pounds, if memory serves me right. From there I had only a short journey into Germany by train.

My intuition had been right. I found my mother far from well. She was in the hands of an able doctor whom I went to see without her knowledge. He was guarded, assuring me that there was no immediate danger, but that in the long run my mother should not continue to live in surroundings which were now painful to her. It was no use my offering not to go back to Scotland. However, we decided that in the autumn when my trainee year was over, and a permanent work permit might not yet be available, we should move to Wiesbaden, an international spa where we could live more anonymously, and it would be a jumping-off ground for emigration the moment the chance came along. The plan comforted us both, yet I spent the radiant summer in an uneasy frame of mind, unable to join in the carefree pleasures of my Scottish contemporaries.

I returned to my mother in September when we were both faced with the emotion-laden task of clearing a house which had been the family home for more than a generation. We only kept enough furniture and household goods to fill the flat Mother had arranged to rent. By October of that year we moved, with a mixture of sadness and relief, leaving behind a place where not so very long ago we had been happy.

There were no goodbyes because most of our friends could not now openly associate with us. It was best to leave quietly, almost unobserved. Our house was being let through a lawyer. On the last morning we walked slowly to the station, and when I turned at our street corner, I somehow knew that this was the definite end of life as I had known it.

Our flat was in a quiet residential part of Wiesbaden. I never liked it but took care to keep my feelings to myself. I felt cut off from my roots, an outcast in a strange and unreal world. In Scotland I had felt that I could grow new roots, but not here. We made few friends. Nobody could be trusted anyway and in some ways the anonymity was comforting. Still, the truth was that we were 'set apart' and our outwardly quiet existence was artificial. In Wiesbaden Nazi excesses were kept at bay because the spa still welcomed many foreign visitors. They had to be given the impression that all was well, and that horror stories they might have heard were nothing but the invention of enemies of the regime.

Efforts by a number of people in Scotland did not secure me a work permit, and time went on drearily. Of course, I could not get work in Germany, but gave my life some sort of purpose by teaching basic English to Jewish youngsters about to emigrate under children's schemes. My mother's health improved slightly, and when my friends suggested that I should visit them again in Scotland, and that my presence might help obtain a permit, I went.

While I was away my mother suffered a heart attack.

Only after much persuasion did she allow a sister-in-law who had been called to her side, to inform me that she had had a bad attack of 'flu'. All the same, I rushed back and found her in a very poor condition. By now hospitals were very reluctant to admit Jews. Also with many Jewish doctors emigrating, there was a shortage of doctors. No hospital would take my mother in, and we had to manage as best we could with a devoted half-Jewish doctor who was allowed to 'associate' with us without hindrance and an equally devoted Catholic nursing sister. For months my mother was very ill. By an irony of fate, when her health was at its lowest, my work permit arrived. I could not even tell her because she would have wanted me to go there and then. After some months my mother had recovered sufficiently for me to tell her about the permit, and she insisted that I should take advantage of the chance to work. She was hopeful; the news had greatly cheered her. In the spring, she said, come what may, she would join me in Scotland. By that time, she thought, she might be well enough to do some kind of light work, and help in building a new life for us both.

Three months after my departure my mother died in a second heart attack.

I was desperate and stunned when the news reached me as only days before I had had a cheerful and cheering letter, telling me how much she looked forward to joining me in the spring. I will never know how much of this was 'acting' on my mother's part or how much she really believed she could overcome her severe difficulties. My only thought now was 'to be near her', to go to her funeral, be close to her in death as I had been in life.

Everybody advised me against going to Germany, but I was determined and at that stage did not mind much what would happen to me. I required a visa which the German consul in Glasgow refused to give. Even though I had not yet formally emigrated, he considered me a 'Jewish emigrant' who had no right to re-enter Germany. I explained the special circumstances but the consul stated adamantly that he could not grant a visa for any reason whatsoever. An Edinburgh legal friend came to my rescue and after two days of struggle and threats that he would take up the matter at once with the German ambassador in London, the consul, still reluctantly, produced the necessary stamp in my passport. The argument which finally persuaded him was that I had no 'J' marked in my passport, the 'J' every Jewish emigrant had entered in his passport by the authorities. In fact, my mother and I had been advised to complete our formal emigration only at the point of her being able to join me. This would not now happen.

In a daze I boarded the night train at Waverley, caught the Channel boat and was met on the other side by my mother's brother who had been alerted to my arrival. It was natural that my mother should be buried by my father's side in the family burial ground in Detmold. There had been no objection to this and my uncle and I travelled through heavy snowstorms to my old home, arriving just in time for the funeral. By coincidence our car reached Detmold's main street for us to see the cortège stop for a moment in front of the house of my childhood. This was a spontaneous act of respect by the driver to whom our family was well known, and I can see him now lifting his top hat for a second before driving on.

I had not realized that almost immediately after my mother's funeral I should have to deal with my family lawyer. He advised me to make definite plans for the future at once. He also said that my presence in Germany would be required for some weeks at least. I was totally confused, and at the moment 'future' meant absolutely nothing to me. I asked for time to think matters over, and told the lawyer next morning that I wanted to return to Scotland and get advice there. He shook his head, but, of course, had to let me go.

My new friends in Scotland were wonderful. They were now divided into two camps: the ones that thought the risk of my returning once more to Germany too great, and the others who felt I ought to save as much of my material possessions as possible. A newly acquired Scottish lawyer, a fine old gentleman, belonged to the latter. Unfortunately, he was completely unaware of the situation inside Germany, and, kindly and fatherly, patted me on the back, assuring me that any international bank could deal with the transfer of my mother's property which was now mine. However, he did do a great deal to strengthen my decision to go to Germany and straighten out things. At that time I was certainly not motivated by materialistic considerations, but was horrified at the thought that strangers, most likely Nazi officials, should go through our family belongings and that many might just be thrown on a bonfire. This I knew to have happened to the belongings of 'stateless' persons. The Nazi authorities now considered me to be in that category. I have always had and still have a very real attachment to chattels, things I have lived with for a very long time. They become more than 'things', take on a personality as, I seem to remember D.H. Lawrence wrote: 'go on glowing for long years....'

I did not wish to go back to my old home but rather wanted to stay in the anonymity of the spa, so I acquired the services of an international lawyer in nearby Frankfurt. This time I was seen off at Waverley by a few friends, mainly customers of the bookshop, who tried, not very successfully, to appear cheerful and hide their concern for me. As the train pulled out of the station, one of them, a well known Edinburgh librarian, waved his arms with a big, if slightly forced, smile and shouted: 'Come back soon, and remember you are very much wanted and needed here.' These words and the man's smiling face were a lifeline in the weeks to come.

Arriving in Germany, I took a room in a small boarding house owned by a French family, and travelled every day to Frankfurt and my lawyer's office. He, himself of 'mixed origin' and preparing to emigrate soon, helped me a lot. Everything from our old house, all so precious to me, particularly our books, was, after detailed inspection by Nazi officials, declared ready for 'overseas transfer'. That is, provided the required rate of *Fluchtsteuer*, a tax arbitrarily set up for emigrants, was paid. As my money or property I left in Germany was 'frozen' anyway, the payment of this tax became a mere formality. The inspection of our household goods was made easier by them having been placed in store when I went to Scotland. At the time Mother had taken rooms in a small private hotel, run by a Russian woman doctor. This, she hoped, would make her joining me in the spring of 1938 easier. Also, she had medical supervision, and a foreign-owned hotel was then a reasonably 'safe' place to be in. She did not live to see her plans come to fruition.

During the three months since I left for Scotland the atmosphere in Germany had certainly become more tense. Fear had spread like an infectious disease. Nobody wanted to talk, and more and more signs were turning up in shop windows, cafés, restaurants and hotels: 'No Jews served'. Luckily I had discovered a small unpretentious café near the railway station where I could have a snack every night, unmolested. I then went back to my room and stayed there. After a little while I noticed that the boarding house proprietors were a little uneasy about me, and with the utmost politeness kept asking when I was going back to Scotland.

I was soon to learn the reason for their concern. People who were paying frequent visits to foreign countries had become suspect to the Secret Police. I was aware that the slightest wrong move could land me in a concentration camp. Yet, somehow I was bent on finishing my self-imposed task and not frightened, even though I avoided the public as much as possible. Then, one evening when I returned to the house, a very pale-looking Madame handed me a letter without a word. On my query she said that a man in black uniform had called several times, and then left the letter about an hour ago. I opened the letter and found that I was to appear at an address – stating the address but not the nature of the place – at eight o'clock next morning. I am not sure what my feelings were; escape never crossed my mind. I certainly did not sleep, but set out in the morning fairly calm, telling myself if this was fate, here it was.

I soon reached the address, and after passing two grim-looking guards who sneeringly told me that I was expected, I was taken to a large room. It was completely empty but for a raised desk, a large portrait of Hitler, and an enormous band covering one whole wall, bearing the slogan: *'Immer ist der Jude dein Feind'* – the Jew is your enemy always. Neither the stage-managed setting nor the slogan upset me. One had become so used to that sort of thing. I calmly waited for what was to happen. Soon enough from a door behind the desk a youngish Gestapo man entered the room. He raised his arm in the Hitler salute to which I did not reply.

He then said he would read out a dossier to me, and I should have to sign it at the end of the proceedings. This dossier, to my astonishment, contained a pretty accurate story of my life, but ended by saying that I had made myself liable to punishment for visiting foreign countries secretly in the course of the last few years. When he had finished, the man handed me the document for signature. In the most courteous way I then explained to him that I could not sign because the remarks about travel were untrue. To my surprise he then asked for my own version which I gave in detail. I added that my plan was to emigrate to Scotland as soon as matters could be – I emphasised this – legally arranged.

The young man thought for a minute, then called in a second man, and asked me to take an oath on what I had said. I did, and he told me that I was free to prepare for my emigration, but that in the meantime the Secret Police had to confiscate my passport. Also, I must daily report at the building, and hand in a written statement about the previous day's activities. Then I was dismissed, wondering what on earth had saved me from 'protective custody'.

I continued with my preparations as before, and for some weeks handed in my reports faithfully. Nothing further happened. Then, one morning, my passport was returned to me, with a note to say that I was now free to leave but not before I had supplied my final report.

Suddenly I panicked.

I wrote my report, spoke to my lawyer over the telephone in guarded language, paid the boarding house for a week, and caught the next train for Aachen and the frontier. I broke my journey for a couple of hours in Cologne from where I posted my report, regretting that I had been unable to hand it in personally.

It would reach the *Gestapo* only when I was safely on the Channel boat. In Aachen an emigration officer told me brusquely – seeing the special 'J' (Jew) stamp now in my passport – that I could never return to Germany. 'That,' I said, 'I can promise with the greatest of pleasure.' I broke my promise only years later, after the defeat of the Nazis in the Second World War, and then only after much persuasion. I felt overjoyed on having crossed the German frontier for the last time.

PART IV

A New Home and a New Life

Chapter 10

Reaction set in once I was on the cross-Channel boat. The elation I had experienced on leaving Germany changed into deep depression. I felt desperately lonely and lost, unable to comprehend how I had got through the the last couple of months and wondering whether it had all been worth it. It might perhaps have been better if the Gestapo had put an end to my life. Who, anyway, cared whether I was alive or dead, least of all myself at the moment. Mechanically I caught the boat train, changed stations in London and arrived in Edinburgh with my spirits at a very low ebb.

Again, everybody there was kind and friendly, and I recognised that in my saner moments. In my more off-balance states I became critical of the cold houses, the solemn drabness and, what then seemed to me the backwardness of much I lived with. I could not understand how people put up with the discomfort of freezing bedrooms or be courageous enough to undress in unheated bathrooms. I never had a bath that winter but just washed 'in bits', turning my nightdress a little up and then down, unable to bear the arctic indoor conditions. My bed-sitter had only a metered gas fire and as I could not afford to feed it with enough shillings to give me comfort, I went to bed early most evenings, dressed in my knitted tobogganning suit: breeches, sweater, scarf, gloves and all. In my innocence I had expected winter sport in Scotland. This was not so. However, my outfit allowed for a comfortable few hours' reading in bed. Being taken out to a concert or play made a welcome break. Plays I enjoyed very much because listening carefully to the dialogue and trying to follow it, trained my ear for colloquial English.

One evening stands out in my memory when a serious young Swiss invited me to a concert. At the end of it he wanted to take me out for a meal. I explained to him the lack of 'night life' in Edinburgh and that at ten o'clock in the evening we could not possibly find food anywhere. In his rather deliberate manner he replied, 'Swiss Calvinism does not consider it sinful to sit and chat over a fondue at midnight.' That was that. All he could do, was to see me home in a taxi. In the privacy of my room I nibbled a biscuit and cheese, an emergency ration which I always kept ready in a tin.

I had no money to buy clothes or anything of consequence. What I earned from bookselling just kept me housed and fed. Yet, I did enjoy walking along Princes Street in my lunch hour to 'window shop'. I admired the beauty of the street and the silhouette of the Old Town but the shops were disappointing, with old-fashioned, overcrowded displays of mostly dowdy clothes. My own clothes, though by now a few years old, were much liked by my women colleagues for their smartness. I created quite a stir when one warm day I turned up in the shop in a white piqué dress and white sandals. Nobody had ever done that before, and when one of the good-humoured porters remarked: 'Good God, lassie, I thought you had come out in your goonie!' I never did again either.

I got on very well with my male and female colleagues at Thin's. One or two of the older employees were interested to hear about my bookselling work on the Continent; so was Ainslie Thin who considered the organisation of the German booktrade and the training of booksellers there exemplary. Through his recommendation, I was invited to speak to young publishers at a meeting of the Publishers Association in London. I was very proud and even now remember the occasion with pleasure. I must have looked very young because one of the audience sought permission to ask, 'Did you start in the cradle?' I had just told my public that I had eleven years of experience in Germany. In fact, I was over thirty.

I saw the Thins at the beginning of every working day. We discussed the day's work or points arising from orders and general correspondence. They were well informed and a pleasure to work with. It was an exceptional honour to be invited to their homes, particularly at Christmas when I was included in the family party. I did not make close friends among the staff but we now and again went in small groups to the pictures on our free Saturday afternoons or had lunch out when our work was finished at the weekend. We saved one and sixpence for a three-course meal, live romantic music included.

During my daily rambles in Princes Street I got used to stopping at the Hanover Street branch of Crawford's restaurants and cafés. For sixpence I could buy myself a sardine on toast and a cup of coffee, served in blue-and-white willow pattern china. Jugs of milk stood on the tables and I could fill up my cup, getting a little extra nourishment for the money I was able to set aside for lunch each day.

My reason knew very well how lucky I was to be in a friendly country, far from a regime which at best would have interned me and in the end almost certainly applied 'the final solution' in the gas chambers of Auschwitz. Yet, a subconscious homesickness, a longing for something which had gone forever, made me irritable when good and well-meaning friends pointed out little 'Continental ways' I had to rid myself of. 'One doesn't shake hands here,' they said. 'Don't hold your fork like a shovel,' and above all it was bad to 'talk shop' or 'make personal remarks'. One elderly hostess quietly rebuked me at a tea party for having admired a lady's dress 'openly'. That was far too personal. I had to learn to make small talk. Nor was I ever to comment on food or drink. Food in the private houses I was invited to was plain but good as in fact it was in my boarding house where the worst was that one could not ask for second helpings. Restaurant food when I had the chance to taste it was, with one or two exceptions, pretty awful. To complain about it was not 'the done thing', I was told, although complaints might have served a useful purpose. However, I suffered silently, remembering my instructions. A Hungarian bookseller friend of mine on a visit north from London did not allow himself inhibitions. When he was served a few lettuce leaves, a slice of sour beetroot and half a semi-ripe tomato without any dressing, masquerading as a salad, he sent it back with the memorable words: 'Waiter!' 'Yes, Sir.' 'Take this to your rabbits.' The face of the waiter spoke volumes.

Once again work proved a great help. I was at home among books and the people who bought them. Some of our librarian customers became friends and mentors. Working with the university booksellers, I was fortunate in having an intelligent and understanding boss. Ainslie Thin stood out among his countrymen in comprehending the German situation as it really was. He and his family lived not very far from my boarding house, and as we both walked to work in the morning, I sometimes had the privilege of a ten minutes' talk with him when we met. It was comforting to know that he fully understood my anxieties which a good few at that time considered groundless, even neurotic. I was fearful about the fate of my relations left behind in Germany and every liberal-thinking person there. I dreaded Hitler's hunger for power and expansion and was altogether apprehensive of the future. There were many among my customers who openly admired the *Führer* for trying to 'put Germany back on its feet'. One lady who did not know German but had recently been to Berlin, assured me that my 'prejudices' against Hitler and his ideas would be swept away by his success. 'In fact, European success,' she added triumphantly. I heard with disgust how Herr von Ribbentrop was lionised at London parties as a hero in the war against Communism. It was often difficult to remain silent, faced with all that enthusiasm about a regime which I knew to be thoroughly evil.

In time, a little stronger in myself and more balanced, I saw the many good sides of my new surroundings. I recollect now how the complete lack of pomposity struck me and the sense of humour of my Scottish colleagues. Sure enough, they did not work half as hard, or concentrate, as I had been used to, but they were happier and more relaxed than their German counterparts. The friendly chatter of tea breaks and the luxury of half days were novelties to me.

I used the unaccustomed freedom of Saturday afternoons for getting to know Edinburgh's surroundings. Sometimes alone, more often in the company of new friends – mostly 'bookish' people I had met in my work, I walked over the Braids, parts of the Pentlands and went, partly by bus, even as far as Quensferry to admire the Forth Bridge. Many a Saturday night I was taken to the Lyceum theatre by a stage-struck librarian to see the Brandon-Thomas company perform. Even though I could not always follow quickly spoken dialogue, I enjoyed the plays.

The height of pleasure was the discovery that for half a crown I could have an hour's riding on the Braid Hills. I saved wherever I could, had a bun and an apple for lunch instead of going to Crawford's. I walked instead of taking the tramcar. This allowed for at least every second Sunday morning indulging my passion for horses. Soon enough, the owner of the stables discovered that I knew a little about horses and I was now and again allowed to help with the grooming or even get an hour's free ride on my own when there was a spare horse which needed exercising. I looked forward eagerly to these Sunday mornings. The rest of the day I usually spent in my room, reading. Although my immediate work dealt with foreign literature only, I wanted to get to know more about English literature and contemporary writing in English. Again, my librarian friend was a great help in recommending books and often lending them to me.

On my first crossing to Antwerp on board the *Grangemouth* I had met an Edinburgh Q.C. and his wife, about to visit their daughter at a Belgian convent school. We had got on well together and they belonged to the precious few who understood the German situation and the menace of Hitler to the whole of Europe. They had taken the address of my boarding house and were not long in inviting me for Sunday dinner after I returned from my journey. This Sunday dinner became a habit and our friendship grew closer as time went by. In the spring of 1938 they suggested that I should leave the boarding house to come and stay with them for a while at their pleasant home in Liberton.

Living in a family, they maintained, would make me feel more at home in my new country, also I should be able to save some money towards the time when my household goods would arrive from Germany. The cost of the shipping was paid out of 'frozen' German funds, but I should have to find ready money for storage and insurance until I could think of a home of my own. My friends were right on both accounts. Insisting that I would only come as a paying guest, I made the move and never regretted it.

As I shared the family's activities in the evenings and at weekends, I no longer felt an outsider and I began to understand much which until then had appeared strange to me. My hostess was a good cook and to sit down to dinner every night in the family circle was a great treat. I shared my room with the daughter of the house, recently returned from her school in Belgium. Younger than myself, she was lively and full of fun, a great companion to have around. The two sons of the family now accompanied me on my Sunday rides when I discovered more and more beauty around me. Some evenings we all went to a close by country pub, with everybody anxious to make me feel one of them. A few tried to teach me the sort of English I could not learn from books, and the muddle that followed through my using terms which I did not fully understand, gave rise to much hilarity. We made excursions into the Borders where for the first time I saw Sir Walter Scott's countryside, and I loved it. Scott had been one of my father's favourite writers so I had been introduced to him in my childhood.

Then one day suddenly I was informed that the container with my goods and chattels had reached Leith docks. My friends eased me through the formalities, found me a storage firm and an insurance company and also introduced me to a bank. At this time my dealings consisted of paying in a pound one week and taking out ten shillings the next. However, some good people managed to get me a few evening pupils for German conversation and their fees – half a crown for an hour – I paid into my acount without ever touching them.

I had now lost almost all touch with Germany. A few young relations had been fortunate to get away – two after spending some time in Buchenwald concentration camp. They were too busy trying to settle in the far corners of the world even to give a thought to writing. Elderly relatives, trapped in Germany, only sent cryptic postcards, saying they were fairly well or mentioning what the weather was like. Obviously they were frightened to convey any real message. Even communications from my Dutch family revealed them to be not as free and easy as they had been only a year or two ago.

New groups of refugees with terrible tales to tell reached Edinburgh during the summer of 1938. They were mostly Austrians who had fled after the *Anschluss*, Hitler's successful annexation of their country in March of that year. With a single theatrical coup he had achieved his ambition of creating the *Grossdeutschland* which he had so constantly referred to in his public outpourings. Among the refugees were a few Germans who had naively considered Austria to be a safe haven. Now some Austrians chose Prague as a place of refuge. Their friends in Britain feared for them as they firmly believed Czechoslovakia to be Hitler's next target. This belief became more general as political awareness grew. Then, on 15th September, came Neville Chamberlain's dramatic flight to Munich, followed by another one to Godesberg and yet another to Munich in late September. The pathetic piece of paper, making hopes rise of 'peace for our time', made me shudder. Every reasonable person wished for peace but I could not see it while the *Führer* remained in power. The distribution of gas masks showed that I was not the only one to distrust appearances. New waves of refugees confirmed my fears that Hitler might well be ready for new 'adventures'. Most of my Scottish friends still considered my apprehension as arising from an anxiety complex created by my recent past.

Soon enough there came news of the terrible *Kristallnacht* when during the night from 9 to 10 November by order of the party, all synagogues in Germany were burnt down, Jews savagely attacked and their shops and houses looted. Many went to concentration camps never to return. For the first time I felt something close to joy that my mother had not lived to see those horrors in Germany and most likely be carted off to a camp herself. When I had emptied my mother's desk after her death I found that she had kept a small file of cuttings concerning Nazi cruelties. They came from foreign newspapers which she had precariously obtained. It was a dangerous thing to have done but quite in keeping with my mother's courage. She undoubtedly thought to make use of this evidence at some future date. Needless to say, I destroyed the file the moment I found it. Many years later I learnt, via the Red Cross, that a number of elderly aunts and uncles were taken to Theresienstadt at the time of the *Kristallnacht*, either to die there or end in the gas chambers of Auschwitz.

I was also to find out that one of my aunts survived miraculously several years later in Theresienstadt. After a rehabilitation period in Switzerland, arranged by Allied organisations, she returned to Munich. There, she found her home destroyed but many of her belongings taken into care by loyal neighbours and friends. She rebuilt her life courageously and enjoyed it for a little while. On a visit after the war I found her reluctant to talk about her internment except that she had worked in camp welfare. This meant recycling the clothes of inmates who had been sent to 'the final solution' at Auschwitz. It was a nightmare experience to recognise old friends and relations from the name tapes on their clothing.

In the autumn of 1938 a combination of lucky circumstances allowed me to become the owner of a top flat, the one-time nursery of a house on the fringe of Edinburgh's New Town. I had not seen any of our belongings for some time now, but the mere thought of living with them – alone – brought back the old depression. Yet, I knew that I could not pay for storage indefinitely and that to accustom myself to the thought of living in the flat was the only sensible thing to do. The flat had been empty for some time, was neglected and in desperate need of cleaning and redecoration. I steeled myself and made the necessary arrangements for the delivery of my goods out of storage. It so happened that at that moment my hosts were going abroad for a month. They proposed to close their house and give me a chance to experiment with the flat. They were, of course, to leave the keys with me, so that I should not feel pushed out. In fact, they fully expected me at least to sleep at their house.

The weekend they departed for Switzerland I went to the flat to try and sort things out a little. I was physically and mentally miserable as I climbed the many steps to the top. Inside, furniture had been put any old way and boxes of linen, china, cutlery, kitchen utensils and, of course, books were piled high. A caretaker from the house next door had been helpful during the arrival of my things when I could not leave work to be on the spot. He had also opened all the boxes to make it easy for me to unpack as and when I was ready to do so.

Now, pulling out something here and there, looking at books and objects I had been familiar with all my life, I cheered up. In an almost magical way 'things' became friends, and suddenly I felt that I could make a home for myself. I took the tram, fetched my suitcase and decided to spend the night at the flat. I somehow managed to make up a bed in the midst of what looked like a furniture store and slept more soundly than I had done for many months. Home was all around me. I had no domestic experience whatsoever, but that Sunday morning memories of my mother turned into happy recollections. I tried to visualise how she would have made order out of chaos.

The electricity had never been cut off and there was water. I could have a cold wash but could not boil a kettle because the continental plugs did not fit. There was no facility for cooking yet. On the Saturday night I had quickly picked up bread, milk, cheese and a pound of apples. I lived happily on my provisions. There was one great blessing though it was also an expensive luxury for me at the time, a telephone. I rang one or two of my friends who were delighted to hear that I had overcome my misgivings, and during the weeks to follow they helped in word and deed. One particularly gallant one – my librarian – arrived one evening while I was up to my eyes in staining floors.

'It's time you had a change,' he said. 'I'm now taking you to a new little restaurant; get changed and be quick about it.' 'I can't go with these hands. They'll not scrub quickly,' I protested. 'In cases like that, charwomen wear gloves,' came the laconic reply.

And go we did and enjoyed ourselves greatly. At the *Apéritif* we were served the best food I had eaten in Edinburgh so far. No wonder, the place was to become the gourmet restaurant of the city, achieving fame during the war when it was frequented by people of many nations.

My flat became very important to me, so much so that I even went there during my short lunch break, just to think over what to do next. The gas cooker was soon connected and I made my first attempts at cooking. The discovery of a bunch of recipes written down by my mother was a great joy. From then on I could conjure up the tastes and smells of my childhood, and feeding myself became easier. My bathroom was not yet properly fitted, and I had a plumber recommended, also a painter who was understanding, willing to do work in instalments as and when I could pay for it. There was no lack of funny incidents during the months of precariously trying to establish myself. A very modern gas hot-water heater was among my household goods, and I naturally wanted it to be put up. The plumber looked at the heater, shook his head and said that I would certainly need the gasboard's permission to install 'yon foreign thing'. I applied to the board, they came to inspect the heater, admired the workmanship of it and explained to the plumber how best to put it up in the bathroom. Once there, it was to supply bath and basin with hot water, also the kitchen sink on the other side of the wall. The officials left and the plumber again sadly shook his head.

'Don't say I didn't warn you. You should use the kitchen fire, just bank it up before you leave in the morning. Forget about yon foreign thing. Because if you don't, you'll wake one morning and find yourself dead.'

However, I persevered and 'yon foreign thing' served me well for many years. The good plumber marvelled at the fact every time he came to the flat for some repair or other.

I was never a good do-it-yourselfer. The society I was brought up in set too great a store by the expert who was expected to do things to perfection. In my young days he actually did, and nothing was less acceptable. As dirty walls and torn wallpapers were horrible eyesores, the painter's arrival could not be delayed. An increasing number of night pupils would make it possible to do at least one room at a time. I was very anxious to get the flat's woodwork out of its liverish-brown appearance. How did I want it, the painter asked. I explained that I should like it all, bit by bit, done in matt ivory paint. The elderly man looked aghast.

'With your permission, Madam,' he said when he had got his breath back, 'that would hardly be respectable, particularly at such a good address.'

This was in Edinburgh in 1938, and I really did not know what the man was talking about. Again I insisted and won. No harm came to the flat, the painter or myself. Years after it was explained to me that in the man's mind light colours and 'places of light virtue' were possibly associated as, indeed, they had been with an older generation. Dark brown only, preferably grained, was considered perfectly respectable.

Overcoming one obstacle after another, I made a real home of my own, still comforted by living with 'things' I had known all my life. I spent evenings sorting out our books, a busman's holiday perhaps, but a happy one.

As I settled in comfortably, it became clear to me that I could not afford to run the flat on my own. Sharing was suggested which at that time was a formidable and frightening thought to me. Though by and large sociable, I have always valued privacy and quietness very highly. However, sharing was a necessity and eventually was to supply me with a number of lifelong friends. When Christmas came, I put up decorations, bought a goose, stuffed it with chestnuts and apples, as Mother had done, and gave my first dinner party. It was a great success.

I was now completely at ease in my work, and English seemed to come naturally. I had sat a 'proficiency exam' for foreigners, and though it was quite a small thing, it gave me a sense of achievement. I also attended Extra Mural University classes in English language and literature. I read a great deal in my spare time and rejoiced when I discovered that it no longer mattered whether a book was written in English or German.

A colleague's brother had a car and I was quite often included in a small family party being taken to the country for afternoon teas. We went to North Berwick and the Berwickshire coast where I, a landlubber, until now, loved watching the changing moods of the sea. I also got to know the broad fields and country lanes of East Lothian and walked in the heather of the Lammermuirs. Affection for the Scottish scene grew steadily within me. Early in 1939 I had saved enough money, mainly through teaching in the evenings, to afford a week's holiday in Perthshire. It was a wonderful experience and I returned to Edinburgh with the definite feeling of coming home.

Chapter 11

Political realities again threatened my budding sense of security. In March 1939 Hitler occupied Czechoslovakia. The Austrian refugees had been only too right. About that time Britain promised to protect the independence of Poland, a country thought by many to be the next target for Hitler's ambitions. Yet, during that summer my work and the little 'play' there was, went on as usual. Most of my colleagues still believed in peace, with the one exception of an elderly man who kept telling me about a visit he and his wife had paid to Hamburg the previous year. At their table in an open-air restaurant some youths had haughtily declared, 'Tell your Englanders that we are only waiting for *'der Tag'* when our *Führer* will lead all Europe, including your islands.' That talk had shocked this particular colleague into realising what might lie ahead, and he kept repeating in disgust: *'Der Tag,, der Tag. . .'*

Nazi propoganda talk of 'the day, the day. . . ' when all Europe would be under the *Führer's* yoke, had had a traumatic effect.

In August we heard about the trial black-out in London and the inevitable semed to come closer. Strangely enough, I who was brought up to hate all war, could not help experiencing a certain satisfaction with what was happening. At long last Hitler was recognised as the common enemy.

Two young women were now sharing my flat but that August they were away on vacation from their colleges. One evening one of them rang from her home on the Banffshire coast to say that her parents did not meantime wish her to return to Edinburgh as war seemed imminent. Then, in the early hours of 1 September German troops invaded Poland. I was in the habit of picking up an evening paper at the railway station, and that evening I saw on the dimly lit platforms queues of women and children, clutching in their hands gas masks and small suitcases, ready for evacuation.

More and more war became a certainty while there were still rumours of renewed peace moves. Concentration on work was pretty hopeless on the Saturday. On Sunday morning one of my flatmates who had returned at the end of her vacation sat with me listening to the wireless. Shortly after eleven o'clock Mr. Chamberlain came on explaining that all efforts at keeping the peace had failed and that we were now at war with Germany. Again, combined with horror and with fear, I could not help experiencing a feeling of elation about fighting for victory over the Nazis and all they stood for.

We began almost at once to make black-out curtains from dark-dyed cotton which I had found among my mother's sewing materials. We had to make safe windows and rooflights. Next day we laid in candles in case of an emergency. At work a few male colleagues were called up straight away and I took over some of their work. One morning the sirens screamed and staff and customers were shepherded into deep old cellars under Edinburgh's North Bridge. Nobody panicked and after a while an elderly professor marched up the stairs, muttering, 'I'm going home, cook won't wait with lunch.' This might be a typical example of British sang froid, only the professor was Belgian by birth. Soon after his exit the all clear sounded and we never knew what had actually caused the alarm in the first place.

In general my daily routine was undisturbed except that for a little while students packed every nook and cranny of my flat. The university hostels for women were requisitioned and the warden, a friend of mine, begged me to house three or four of her girls until more permanent accommodation could be found.

With three bedrooms in the flat I was glad that I could help. In addition to the existing beds, we quickly made up two settees and everybody was comfortably housed. As the students had a shorter working day, they offered to cook during the week while I did the cooking at weekends. At that stage it was quite a jolly war as preparing meals and running the house was done with much chat and laughter. We were almost sorry when after a week or two accommodation was found for the students and the flat seemed unusually quiet.

It came as a great shock to me when about the middle of September I was called before a tribunal. Through interrupting my stay in Britain during my mother's illness and at the the time of her death, I had not the five years of permanent residence required before application for naturalisation could be made. Only refugees of importance in the arts, science and industry had received British citizenship – ex gratia – at the outbreak of war. Technically I was still German and an 'enemy alien'. However the tribunal seemed just a formal matter and brought no particular hardship. If memory serves me right, I had to give up a bicycle – which I never possessed anyhow – my small camera and a wireless set, neither of great importance to me. I never liked taking photographs as 'taking pictures' seemed to interfere with the pictures I formed in my mind and remembered. This is still true now. Also, the written or printed word leaves a better impression with me than the second-hand experience of radio or television.

My two flatmates being back at their studies and with me again, working and social life went on much as usual and nowhere was I shown the slightest hostility. The winter of the 'phoney war' caused little discomfort. My eyesight, never very good in the dark, made me stagger a little coming back from my work in the black-out. Soon enough I got used to the dim, blue lights and for the first time the moon and stars became distinct guides in the city landscape.

Bad news came from Poland. The army and airforce had collapsed, leaving the country open to threats from East and West. Depressing as this was, Poland was far away and Hitler's further gains seemed of no immediate threat. There was activity at sea, with the cheerful news of the sinking of the *Graf Spee* after the earlier loss of the *Royal Oak*. Many still believed that by the spring of 1940 the war would be over and won.

Run rabbit run—— and *The Siegfried Line* were hummed and whistled at all hours. A friend who was now an Air Raid Warden came in after a night's duty to have breakfast with us, entertaining us with tales of his training in dealing with 'mock casualties'. The worst genuine casualty had been a bleeding nose through coming into close touch with a tin helmet. Everything seemed quite unreal. Then, in April 1940 the Germans marched through Denmark to Norway. I heard through Swiss relations that a cousin in Copenhagen with his young wife had escaped across the Sund to Sweden. Not long after, Hitler's forces overran Belgium and Holland, and the fate of my family there deeply worried me.

It was at that time that a young psychologist in Edinburgh who later on came to prominence in his profession, insisted that in the short time between being awake and falling asleep when horror thoughts kept coming to my mind, I must adopt a 'safety device'. The one he suggested was picturing the fire curtain in a theatre and literally 'seeing' it come down over my thoughts. I did try and it helped. It has done so often since.

I had always been a great admirer of Churchill, not least for what I believed to be his recognition of the German situation long before others. Helped by Hitler's rapid and terrifying successes, Churchill was swept into power. I was cheered, confident that with him at the helm we would come to grips with the evil and destroy it eventually.

Meantime news from the Continent was increasingly bad as the *Blitzkrieg* continued. There was a feeling of tension about and once again my colleagues went out of their way to show me friendliness. On the evening of 10th June a few of them invited me to join them for a swim in Portobello Pool. As a special treat we went back via Leith Walk where at a small Italian café we got an omelette, toast and coffee for one shilling and sixpence. As we were nearing the place we heard shouting and the noise of breaking glass. A mob was storming Italian cafés and ice-cream parlours.

Mussolini had declared war on the Allies.

I was shocked because I had been convinced that that sort of thing could never happen in Britain. Ghosts from the brutal past filled my dreams that night.

Next morning at work faces were glum when, with troops close to the Channel ports, a direct German threat to Britain and a possible invasion loomed large in everybody's mind. Waves of hysterical xenophia found expression in some papers. All aliens were suspect. 'Intern the lot,' it was urged. Where would all the German refugees stand? Would they consider their 'Fatherland' first in the event of an invasion, I was asked? My assurance that they would be more likely to be shot by Hitler's soldiers seemed unconvincing.

As stress built up, Ainslie Thin called me for a private talk. He thought, he said, it was his duty to warn me that Edinburgh might become an area where 'enemy aliens' would not be permitted to stay. I was no doubt aware of the seriousness of the situation but should not forget over the general unease to remember my own very special position. Should an emergency arise, he would contact a bookseller colleague in a 'free' zone where, he had already been assured, I could work while the war lasted. He thought it wise for me to contact my lawyer now in case my flat had to be let.

He stressed that all this was guesswork, yet well worth thinking about. I thanked him and left his office in a daze. For the second time the bottom seemed to drop out of my world.

And drop it did, with a vengeance.

On a fine summer's evening I was sitting at supper when the doorbell rang. Outside stood a tall policeman who in the most courteous manner informed me that I was required to attend a tribunal early next morning. Taken aback, I stammered that I had been at a tribunal six months ago. The policeman shook his head, and looking down from his great height, he said, rather pityingly I thought later, 'Sorry, Madam, I am only here to carry out instructions. Good night.'

'Good night,' was easier said than done. I telephoned Ainslie Thin who did not seem very surprised but assured me that I had absolutely nothing to fear. He would, of course, accompany me as he had done to the first tribunal. That night I was sleepless and fretful. I was glad to see the daylight, got hastily dressed and left for the courts.

We had not long to wait before my name was called. After a few encouraging words from my boss I was faced with the tribunal, three or four men and one woman. I felt much calmer than during the night as I answered questions to the best of my ability, some of them distinctly puzzling.

How was it, the tribunal wanted to know, that I maintained my flat was furnished with my mother's household belongings when, in fact, I had a refrigerator. Was this not odd in view of the fact that my parents were married in 1903? I explained that naturally my mother had kept the household up to date and had quite a few years ago traded in her old ice-box for a refrigerator.

Even during the tribunal the thought of hysterical 'informers' crossed my mind. How else could they have known what kitchen equipment I used? There were other perplexing questions, and only with hindsight do I feel that they tried to establish 'hidden sources of income' which allowed for luxuries well beyond my stated income. Extra income would certainly be suspect at a time when rumours about a Fifth Column were influencing public thinking and putting sinister meanings into innocent facts. After less than an hour the tribunal withdrew for their decision.

They returned after a few minutes, and to this very day their verdict rings in my ears; 'We have considered your case and we have decided that you should be interned.'

I was flattened, unable to say a word while Ainslie Thin appeared to be arguing my case. However, in next to no time I was ushered out of the room and into a police car. There, a woman official told me that we were going to pick up a few things at my flat before proceeding to my temporary place of internment. As we arrived my flatmates were aghast and burst into tears. Then my cool façade collapsed. I flopped into a chair and wept and wept. It took my 'guardian' all her time to calm me sufficiently to be able to pack a few things hastily into a small suitcase.

Ten minutes later I was delivered to Saughton Prison.

All I remember of that evening is the sound of the big key turning in the door of my cell. Dead tired I fell into an uneasy sleep with constant dreams of my mother and my saying: 'I should have never left you. There is no difference between being called 'a dirty Jew' in Germany and 'a filthy German' here. Pray for me to die...'

In the morning a warder opened the door and showed me the washing facilities: a row of small sinks, every one in turn to be used by a woman prisoner. I took the first one available next to a very pretty red-haired girl. 'Morning, dear,' she said. 'What are you in for?' When I told her, she replied, 'That's nothing, I did away with my baby. What else could I do?'

In a strange way I felt much better after that short talk. There were human problems worse than mine. I even ate my breakfast bowl of porridge. Later on we were given what was half a pep talk and half an apology. Accommodation in prison, we were told, was an emergency measure since no other housing was available. Soon we would be sorted out according to our status as internees.

This did nothing to gladden my heart.

In the course of the next day I met some thirty or forty women held in the same way as myself. Sharing our misery during short walks in the prison yard did help. One of these women I knew well. In fact, she had been one of the first people I met on my arrival in Scotland. She was the secretary of a well known Jewish professor from Berlin. When he was hounded out of Germany she voluntarily followed him into exile. An ardent anti-Nazi, she was as unhappy as I was in our present position.

During the next few days we were given little or no news but were allowed a few visits by ministers and Edinburgh's rabbi. They all spoke of the seriousness of the situation – of which we were all too aware – ours being a small part of it. It was well meant but cold comfort, and the announcement of our imminent departure to a more permanent place came almost as a relief.

We were taken to Waverley Station and from there travelled into the unknown. I was too exhausted even to notice where we eventually stopped. Also, by that time, all station signs had been removed in case of an emergency. It must have been somewhere north of Liverpool where we were taken to a large disused warehouse to bed down for the night on thick, dirty blankets. Most internees did not undress but I was so weary that I pulled a pair of pyjamas out of my case, stretched on the doubtful blanket and slept through the whole long night, relieved not to hear a key turning in the door. In the morning we were loaded on to a boat, rumoured to be bound for the Isle of Man. We journeyed slowly and carefully, obviously to avoid mines, and arrived in Douglas. There a committee of officials awaited our arrival. Amongst them I suddenly recognised my university hostel warden friend from Edinburgh. She came towards me and for a short moment we fell around each other's necks and cried. She had to get back quickly to her allotted place, not before whispering in my ear: 'I can't get you out of this. But I'll think, and see how I can help.'

The whole place teemed with women from all over the British Isles. I managed to stick to my Edinburgh friend and, together with others, we were billeted in a peace-time boarding house, four or five women to a room. Our tough-looking landlady turned out to have the proverbial heart of gold. She sympathised with us, served simple, decent food and kept her house spotlessly clean.

The horror was that we were mixed with genuine Nazis. Whether they were actual spies I don't know but I rather doubt it. There were, however, a great number of German and Austrian domestics and hotel staff who bragged openly: *'Mein Schatz ist ein Brauner. Die werden's schon schaffen, wart' nur ab.'* They declared to all and sundry that they were expecting the arrival of their Brown Shirt sweethearts in the British Isles any moment now. One of them shared our room and could not be stopped chattering in spite of our ice-cold silence. In the end she was firmly rebuked by a tall aristocratic German who abused 'the little jumped-up painter from Austria.' This pretty and elegant blonde claimed to have connections in high places both in Britain and the United States. In fact, she said she had been on the point of leaving for America when she was interned. And sure enough, she was soon released to go there.

When rumours of German successes reached the camp the Nazis cheered openly, increasing the distress of the majority of the internees. Tales of suicides in the men's camp circulated freely, and like so many other wild stories could not, of course, be verified.

One, alas, turned out to be only too true; the sinking of the *Arandora Star*, carrying internees on the way to Canada. Husbands, brothers and sons of women in the camp were involved in the tragedy, including Italians whose families had lived in Britain for several generations, but had not bothered to get naturalised. I knew none of these women but their grief distressed me and I felt sympathy for the innocent victims. The sad incident possibly saved the rest of us from being transported overseas.

Meantime, days on the Isle of Man went by in an unreal haze. Many internees settled into an inevitable kind of holiday life. They attended classes arranged for them and took walks within the given limits. Somehow, I was unable to join them. I was deeply distressed about being shut away, superfluous at a time when I felt I might have been useful to my new country, even if in a small way. During August, when the Battle of Britain was at its height, there were a good few who felt privileged 'being away from it all', as they liked to call it. To me it seemed all wrong.

Because of the lack of real news, August and September of 1940 were full of frightening tales: barges were said to be concentrating on the Channel coast, parachutists had landed and bodies of German soldiers were seen floating in coastal waters. It was at this time of great stress that my university warden friend called me to her office to make a proposal which held comfort. Books supplied by charitable institutions and by individuals for the use of internees were accumulating. Would I be willing – with the permission of the Home Office but without pay – to organise the library and then run it? I agreed at once, delighted at the prospect of something to fill the vacant and depressing hours. I was allowed to have an assistant of my own choice. I suggested my Edinburgh internee friend who proved acceptable. We were given an office, began eagerly to catalogue and card-index the books and were soon open for business. We had hundreds of readers, among them were some famous European names, and our stock of books increased all the time. Access to a great lot of reading material was a blessing in itself, together with set hours of work every day.

In the autumn of 1940 a friend of mine was allowed to send me a subscription to *The New Statesman*. It was a boon to have real news instead of rumours. Now and again opinions were expressed, showing concern about refugee internees. This, too, spelt comfort. There were also vague reports of resistance inside Germany. Alas, my first-hand knowledge of the terror prevailing there made me fear that chances of success would be very slight.

In time I received more letters from friends and also heard that some, nobody more eagerly than my boss, had made applications for my release. I got to know then who my real friends were. A few remained silent, not wishing to be involved with 'a suspect'. I became cynical about these 'friends', determined to cut them out of my life should I survive the present situation. Weeks and months went by with not much to distinguish one from another.

A pleasant surprise came one day when I was asked to appear at the camp office. I was told that in recognition of the work we were doing, my assistant and I would be moved to private quarters. It was a marvellous reward and we at once packed our bits and pieces and became the only 'guests' at the house of two elderly ladies. We received no preferential treatment but with pleasant surroundings and no other internees in the house, the privacy was very soothing.

In the spring of 1941 there were many cases of 'flu and respiratory infections in the camp. Though usually not given to colds, I became an easy victim in my low state of body and mind. My companion had to go alone to look after our readers while I lay in bed, unable to eat, listless and feverish. My friend insisted that a doctor should see me, but – to my great relief, because I was fearful of being taken to hospital – camp doctors were overworked and nobody ever appeared. A fellow internee, a nurse by profession, looked in to take my temperature and confirmed that with warmth and rest I should soon be all right. Our good hostesses brought me hot water and honey and in general showed friendly concern. After a week or so I staggered to my feet and was astonished that I could walk only a few steps on the nurse's arm. About that time the news of Rudolf Hess's landing in Scotland came through and one paper reported that he had been given chicken and rice on arrival. How I envied him. My 'flu or whatever it was had left me with a nausea which made it difficult to face ordinary food. Chicken and rice would just have been fine, but I recovered in time even without it.

May went into June before I got my full strength back. By the end of that month a little hope was kindled by the news that Hitler's armies had marched into Russia, no doubt making the Third Reich more vulnerable. Friends in their letters made encouraging remarks about the release of refugees being speeded up. It would, however, they thought, be difficult to return to Edinburgh which remained a 'protected area'. I read similar sentiments into careful remarks made occasionally by Home Office employees with whom I came into contact throught my library work. I kept waiting for a sign. Then, suddenly in early July, quite unexpectedly, I was informed that an order for my release had come through. I was allowed to return to Edinburgh with only two others: one, my friend who had at long last given in to the wooing of her much older employer and was to marry him soon after her return. The other was a young woman whose Scottish mother – her German father had long since died – lived in Edinburgh. It was unbelievable, and I was so dizzy with excitement that I could hardly pack my small suitcase and make ready for the train journey. The camp office had telephoned my lawyer who informed the tenants of my flat of my impending arrival.

Chapter 12

My two companions were met at Waverley Station while I stood alone, free for the first time in thirteen months, facing what suddenly seemed to me a hostile world. I did not board a tram for fear that anybody should recognise me and take me for a returned 'spy'. Rather I walked to Edinburgh's West End and then climbed to my flat, my heart beating furiously. My tenants were friendly enough although naturally a little taken aback with my sudden arrival. Fortunately, my lawyer had kept my own sitting-room locked during the various tenancies in my absence. I made myself comfortable as best I could and telephoned my boss at once, anxious to thank him for all he had done and said I wanted to begin work as soon as possible. He welcomed me wholeheartedly but I could trace a hint of uneasiness in his voice when he invited me to come to dinner with the family the next evening.

I was warmly welcomed at the Thin's house that night, but it soon emerged that there were elements of the staff in the bookshop who now refused to work beside 'a German'. It was considered expedient to give the matter a little time to settle.

I walked home from the south side of Edinburgh, lonely and dispirited. Again, I felt, I was set apart. Also, I had very little money as during the year of internment I had used my small reserves for necessary expenses. Rent received from tenants had just been sufficient to pay a lawyer's fees, rates, and some necessary maintenance. Next day I was invited to dinner by my internee friend and her fiancé. They were sorry to hear about my difficulties and the professor asked whether, with spare time on my hands, I would be willing to translate into English a scientific report he had written in German. This was to be done on a strictly business basis. I agreed gladly, assuring myself of a small income during the next few weeks.

Life in general had become a good deal harder during my absence from home. Rationing was tighter and the range of goods in the shops had become smaller. To begin with I hated shopping as the trauma of being 'a suspect' was still with me. Then, one day I plucked up courage to go into my butcher's in George Street. Charlie, the young manager leapt forward, flung his arms round me and said, 'Welcome home, dear, I believe they interned you. That was a daft-like thing to do. Now tell me what I can do for you.' This wonderful and spontaneous gesture did me no end of good. In fact, it was therapeutic. I began shopping as if nothing had ever happened.

From day to day I hoped for better and definite news from my place of work. Alas, nothing happened. Vaguely I put out feelers in other directions but there appeared no opening for me. Though labour was in short supply I remained redundant and downcast. I began to wonder whether I might be able to help the war effort in a direct way by finding a place in the forces. An interview, however, revealed that because of my background I would most likely end up peeling potatoes in an army kitchen. The interviewer smiled kindly, saying, 'I'm afraid I would think that rather a waste.' I agreed and left.

A friend was anxious to stay with me again at the flat and as I needed more living space, I gave notice to my tenants, a military man and his wife. They found a suitable place fairly quickly and I got my own small bedroom back while my friend returned to the other. Just then I made the acquaintance of a young publisher whose home was bombed in London. Her firm's offices were destroyed also and she was now working in the same publisher's Edinburgh branch. We soon found out that we had lots of interests in common and as she was looking for a room, she joined us in the flat. We made a happy threesome and through their contributions I was able to meet the expenses of the flat.

Some months had passed since my return home when one day I was told by a friend that Mr. William Y. Darling had taken over the old-established booksellers, Robert Grant and Son, neighbours to his own ladies' emporium in Princes Street and model for *The Bankrupt Bookseller* of Will Y. Darling's writings. Mr. Darling himself was one of Edinburgh's most colourful personalities, about to become the city's Lord Provost. It was conveyed to me that he had made discreet enquiries as to my availability to assist him in his new enterprise. I was startled, flattered but also confused. I had deep loyalty to my old employer, but was naturally tempted to explore a most interesting opportunity. It was left to me to telephone Mr. Darling should I be willing to have an informal discussion. After two days and two – almost sleepless – nights I made the necessary appointment.

In his small office high above Princes Street I met the man whom I recognised as one of the most flamboyant I had ever met and later came to regard as one of the most understanding and sensitive of human beings. Dressed in a morning suit with intensely striped trousers and wearing a broad bow tie, he greeted me like an old friend, telling me that he knew my story pretty well. He needed no references but wanted to know if I was interested in becoming his personal assistant in the job, in what he called, 'moving from lingerie to literature'. After an adventurous early life and seeing active service in the First World War, he had settled in his uncle's Edinburgh business and had become, what he called, a silk mercer. Friendly relations with his neighbour and his great interest in literature and the arts had led to his latest enterprise. As civic duties were bound to take much of his time, he wanted a deputy in the firm, willing and able to take responsibility and re-establish good contacts with publishers after Grant's financial difficulties.

I told Mr. Darling how pleased and honoured I was by his offer but that I found the decision difficult because of my attachment to my old place of work. He then stressed that he wished my decision to be absolutely free and well considered, not determined by my present situation. He would gladly give me another day or two to think matters over. I left him, grateful for his sympathy.

It was Thursday. That night I saw friends who thought it only sensible for me to accept. I felt myself that this would not be just a way out of a precarious position but that working as Darling's personal assistant was opening completely new prospects. This consideration tipped the balance. On Friday I wrote my letter of acceptance.

On the Saturday morning Ainslie Thin informed me that, all difficulties overcome, I could resume work in my department now. I was distressed but unable to do anything about it as I had given my word to Will Y. Darling. I wrote to Mr. Thin and got a letter back which I cherished. He fully understood but made it clear that, while wishing me well, he meant 'Au revoir' and not 'Good-bye'. There and then I decided that, my job for Will Y. Darling done satisfactorily and the war over, I would return to Thin's. Seven years later I carried out my decision.

Meantime, during a second interview, Mr. Darling paid me a substantial cheque for writing him a report on the booktrade in Scotland as I saw it. He was, no doubt, interested in the subject but it was also a generous gesture to keep me going for a few weeks until I was to start my work for Grant's.

At last I stood at the beginning of seven happy and interesting years in the midst of the darkness of war. Apart from my general duties of establishing good relations, particularly with London publishers, I was to make a neglected, dusty basement under Grant's Princes Street premises into an art department. We were to stock a good selection of art books together with prints, all kinds of reproductions and art cards. We eventually expanded into having small exhibitions by Scottish artists and sold quite a few paintings, woodcuts and etchings.

It was a task after my liking. It also meant that quite soon I should have to travel to London to try and see how I could stock my new department. With paper rationed to publishers and millions of books and prints destroyed in the Blitz, acquiring sufficient stock was difficult. Just waiting for publishers' representatives to call was not enough. To be on the spot where books were produced was important and I began regular journeys south in an effort to lay my hands on as many new books as possible, spending equal time foraging for second-hand ones. Some publishers and wholesalers from the City had lost most of their stocks but kept salvaged books in huge piles in premises in relatively safer parts of London. They allowed me access to these hunting grounds. Dressed in overalls against rubble and dampness, I knelt in candle-lit cellars and in store rooms, sometimes finding real treasures among heaps of stuff, ravaged by fire and water. One of the strangest experiences was finding a volume of a well known German history of costume. Shortly before the war I had – after much searching in the trade papers – found an incomplete set of this rather rare work for a customer who required it for his research. Volume three was missing in the set and the customer rather grudgingly accepted that under the circumstances he had better take the incomplete set. He kept impressing on me that he hoped I would continue searching for the missing volume. I agreed to appease him, fully aware that there was little chance of finding it. Then, among hundreds of Blitz-damaged books I saw the very volume sticking out from a large pile. It was easily recognised by its violet-coloured art-nouveau binding. The moment the book came north I informed my customer, Patrick Murray, a discerning bibliophile, later to become the founder and curator of the Edinburgh Museum of Childhood. His joy was as great as his surprise. Neither of us ever stopped wondering about the volume's adventurous journey to the salvage heap.

Now and again during my stays in London I had the chance of attending meetings of the Publishers Association. There I saw many of the great names in publishing of the period. The Unwins, Michael Joseph, the Harraps, leading men in Fabers', the Studio and many others. The man who became Sir Allen Lane had just begun his incredible Penguin venture. They all made me very welcome and without exception were keenly interested to hear about my early training in Germany. Most of them had known the German booktrade and its centre, Leipzig, from personal experience in pre-Nazi days. They admired the organisation and the way young people were prepared for their 'trade' in an all-round manner.

My London nights were often interrupted by air-raids alarms and having to go down to shelters though I never experienced a heavy raid. I admired the courage and the cockney wit of many of the people I met.

In Edinburgh we led a comparatively sheltered life with nothing worse to bear than rationing and the shortage of much we had thought indispensable in times of peace. The shortage of things to buy as gifts made the print and picture business boom. We found a framer who had secured good stocks of beading and were fortunate in getting prints framed in large numbers. They sold as quickly as we could supply them.

By now our public was very international through the arrival of new refugees and particularly through members of the allied forces. French sailors with pompoms on their berets, tall, lanky G.I.s and a medley of foreigners from the Pioneer Corps mingled daily with the Edinburgh crowds. Polish officers formed the greatest portion of our foreign customers for books and prints. Their colourful uniforms, their precise military bearing and gallantry established them as favourites with the ladies. They were dinner guests in many households, often repaying hospitality with handsome presents of books or prints.

Though our basement was neither well-lit nor heated, it often became a welcome refuge for elderly ladies out shopping in the cold winters of the war. They got great pleasure from looking at our walls of colourful pictures and the visits of some of them were not without humour. I wore smocks at the time to save my clothes from the inevitable dust of a bookshop. One of the old dears, taking my smock for an artist's outfit, told me that she found it quite remarkable that I could 'paint' all these pictures in the time saved from working in the shop.

Another old lady told me that she like *The Harbour of Delft* because she and her late husband had travelled in Holland many years ago and the picture brought back many happy memories. 'But,' she added pensively, 'I remember the harbour with more of a blue sky. Could you tell the painter when he comes in to do me one with a brighter sky. I would be sure to buy it then.'

With Vermeer dead for over two hundred years this was rather a tall order.

Another younger customer confided in us that she was marrying 'the gent' to whom she had been a housekeeper for twenty years. They were at present redecorating the house and she fancied a few of our pictures. But, she thought, in view of 'the gent' it would be more proper to have the classical figures in the picture 'dressed somehow'.

A very young and rather superior customer asked for a book for her naval fiancé, *The Donkey's Coat*. When I looked puzzled, she added disdainfully: 'You ought to know it; it's a famous Spanish classic.' Only then, and very slowly, the thought of *Don Quixote* dawned on me. Selling books and prints is not without its lighter moments.

After some training in one of Edinburgh's West End lanes, lying full length, flat on my tummy, holding a pump and surrounded by smoke, I now became a fully fledged fire fighter, complete with steel helmet. The duty rota required my services once a week, together with two men and another woman, all employees of Grant's or Darling's, who for fire fighting purposes counted as one firm. In fact, a hole in the wall now united the two firms and there was ample space to accommodate males and females in widely separated parts of the building. The fact of not fraternising during duty hours was firmly impressed upon us. We had camp beds on which we were to rest only, never sleep. I am afraid I dozed off many a time. How I could have coped with a pump on a slithery roof, I didn't dare think. Fortunately the need never arose. One night a week a flatmate and I acted as waitresses in the Women's Services Club. We felt we were doing something to help the war effort and were fortunate in being able to buy our supper of toast and sausages that night off the ration. The war work I enjoyed most was doing some interpreting and translation in the Allied Information Office.

While gradually establishing my place in a new country, I was acutely aware that there were still thousands of 'displaced' people floating uneasily in alien surroundings. I made it my job to single out a few of them and help in my own small way. My flatmate was a keen supporter. Through the agency of the Victoria League we obtained the names of members of the Pioneer Corps and of Overseas personnel for whom we arranged tea parties on Sunday afternoons and on special holidays. They were truly international affairs and, in spite of some language barriers, became the starting point for many a lasting friendship. I can see now the very young Australian soldier at a Christmas party kissing an equally young refugee from Central Europe, and I saw her smile for the first time. A Czech, now serving with the British forces, refused to leave after a Hogmanay party because, he explained, it was considered unlucky in his home country to leave on that night before daybreak. He would just sit in his chair, he said. 'Not be any trouble,' he added. However, we decided to make up a bed for him and my flatmate – taller than myself – offered him a pair of pyjamas. They were the then fashionable 'flamingo-red'. That autumn we had dipped all our rather shabby underwear in bramble juice to freshen it up. There he was, a soldier in his greatcoat walking down the corridor, the flamingo pants dangling round his ankles, deploring the fact that all the comfort we offered him was a hot-water bottle.

Children rescued from Belsen were established in a small country house near Edinburgh for a period of recovery and re-adaptation. We were given permission to visit them at weekends. Quite often we travelled on country buses, laden with cakes and little red jellies precariously made from ration ingredients which we hoarded for the purpose. We were always accompanied by an 'entertainer', someone found among our friends, willing and able to perform before this pitiful assembly of youngsters. A puppeteer proved very popular, quickly establishing rapport with his audience. His humour penetrated distrust and stolid silences. It was rewarding to watch these sad children gradually turn into normal young people, eventually to find permanent homes in this country or overseas.

During his term as Lord Provost of the city of Edinburgh Sir William Darling, as he now was, let me share now and again in the social functions which his office demanded. His charming, handsome wife, Olive, was naturally tired at times of the many calls upon her time as Lady Provost. This might result in a sudden telephone call: 'Mike,' Sir William's short for Michaelis, 'the Lady Provost is indisposed – that does not mean she is ill – but she is not disposed to attend the firewatchers' tea party this afternoon. Will you come?'

I always agreed, not just for the honour of being by Sir William's side but equally for the sheer pleasure his witty badinage and his often surprising actions supplied. He disliked smugness, complacency and better-than-thou attitudes. One Saturday afternoon when faced with a particularly dull lot of do-gooders he was told to his horror that after his speech and the usual bun fight, the well-into-middle-age audience were to play a few indoor games involving 'affinity cards'. He looked appalled, but rose to his feet and gave one of his excellent war-effort speeches. About to finish he added as a kind of afterthought, 'I am told to ask you, ladies, to have your virginity – I beg your pardon – affinity cards ready for the games to begin now.' He left a dazed and silent audience.

Chapter 13

Early in May 1945 news came through of the surrender of the German forces in Europe. The longed-for day had arrived: the war in Europe was over and Hitler's Germany totally defeated. In spite of inner joy I was unable to join in noisy celebrations, experiencing a kind of numbness. One night friends took me out to dinner and we drank to the memory of all Hitler's victims during and before the war.

With the war against Germany over and a greater sense of security this brought along, one neurotic fear kept gnawing at me: Britain would now want to send all foreigners back to where they had come from. It was a completely silly idea but I could not rid myself of it. In his very perceptive way Sir William Darling sensed my anxieties, pooh-poohed them and reassured me in every possible way. After he had become an M.P. it was his habit to invite me to lunch at the House of Commons every time I was in London. I enjoyed these occasions greatly, honoured to be Sir William's guest. One of them I have every reason to remember more than the rest.

Not long after V.E. Day Will Y. Darling proudly offered me the first Camembert which had been flown over from France. We had reached the coffee stage when Sir William spotted Churchill carrying a briefcase under one arm and a cup of coffee in his free hand.

'I'll call Winnie over,' Sir William said. The two men were old friends and had, I believe, similar temperaments. I was flabbergasted, wishing the ground would swallow me up. However, before I could even open my mouth we were joined by Churchill. He was much smaller than I had pictured him, wearing a smart navy-blue suit and the usual polka-dotted bow tie. In no time I was introduced to the great man, Will Y. Darling telling him at the time of, what he called, 'the accident of my birth' and the fears I harboured. Churchill looked at me with the most engaging roguish smile, laid his hand on my shoulder and said, 'And we won't send her back, I am sure.' Then, finishing his coffee, he left us with a cheerful wave.

Sir William went back to the Chamber and I kept my next appointment with a publisher still dizzy with excitement.

In August 1945 the horrors of Hiroshima and Nagasaki finally ended the war in the East. World War II was finally at an end.

My naturalisation eventually came through in 1947. I had at long last achieved my wish of becoming a British subject, able to apply for a passport. It meant much to me, but not in terms of foreign travel. My earlier experiences had made for a phobia: I never wanted to set foot on the Continent again, let alone travel to Germany. Now I was suddenly asked by Sir William to attend the first big international meeting of publishers and booksellers after the war. It was to be held at St. Gallen in Switzerland. I explained my feelings to Will Y. and, as always, he was understanding but begged me to think the matter over. I was wrong, he thought, to go through life with a complex. Travel would offer me so much in years to come.

He was right.

It took a few weeks of thinking and discussion with good friends before I came round to agreeing. Not long after, I travelled to Switzerland with my brand-new British passport.

It was strange at first to be in a country where everything was plentiful. I could not eat the big meals offered, limiting myself to soup and one course. I simply had no room for more.

It was wonderful to see old friends and colleagues again, many of whom had narrowly escaped death under the Nazis. They were reluctant to talk about their experiences, but I remember the story of one man, younger than the rest. He was rounded up with his parents during the infamous *Kristallnacht* and sent off to Poland. Not long after their arrival the whole group was placed in front of a firing squad, the boy among them. The command to fire was about to be given when an S.A. man rushed forward, pulling the young man out of line, shouting, 'You are not to die, you are the image of my younger brother.' Commandeering an army vehicle, the S.A. man took the boy blindfold to a hideout. Next morning this turned out to be a remote farm where the Polish farmer explained in broken German that the boy was to work among his labourers and stay until the end of the war. He was well treated all the time but eventually followed the Russian troops back into Germany. Nobody knew what happened to his saviour.

Years after I heard that the man I met in St. Gallen, then in training to be a publisher as his father had been, had committed suicide. His memories proved too much to live with.

I continued to Paris, buying books and arranging for the first small exhibition of French books to come to Scotland after the war. Being in Paris was like walking on air. Warm sunshine and the scent of lime blossom filled my heart with joy, even though I wore the most ghastly utility tweed suit and must have looked like a small square clothes pole. Strangely enough my French appeared to have taken on an English accent because everyone greeted me as coming from the nation of their 'liberators'. Even the chambermaid insisted on washing my blouses free of charge, saying that there was so much to thank the British for.

At long last, I felt that I belonged.

In the summer of 1948 I began to be restless, feeling increasingly that the time had come for me to return to Thin's and my more specialised work with foreign books. It was difficult to speak to Sir William about my plans. However, he fully understood and put me at ease saying, 'I knew, Mike, that some day you would get tired of the city lights and would want to return to a more scholarly atmosphere.' The day after he presented me with a copy of his book *The Bankrupt Bookseller*, inscribed; 'For Ruth Michaelis Jena with many happy and inspiring recollections of dark and difficult days from Will Y. Darling less a Bankrupt Bookseller from knowing her. 1948.' It was a typical gesture.

In October 1948 I went back to Thin's Foreign Department. It was like coming home and I was welcomed by owners and staff and happily by my librarian friends. They were particularly pleased with my return because they knew from previous experience that my contacts abroad might help in obtaining parts of specialised periodicals missing through the war. In my early years with Thin's I had made up sets which had been incomplete since the First War. Through the destruction of so much civilian propety during the Second War many more parts were lost forever. In the course of two years I succeeded in tracing and buying up a good few, often from the most unlikely sources. I went to Scandinavia and Italy looking for desiderata and to replenish meagre stocks.

In 1950 Mr. Thin suggested that it might be a good idea to travel to Germany in an effort to find more material on the spot. Also, the Frankfurt Book Fair was now an important market for books and meeting place for bookmen. The thought of travelling to Germany still horrified me. But, as in 1947, when my reluctance to go to the Continent was eventually overcome, this time, too, there were many friends begging me to go in order to get over the past. Also, while most members of my Dutch family were dead, one cousin had survived Ravensbrück concentration camp and was anxious to see me. I flew to Amsterdam where we had a strange reunion, happy and sad at one and the same time. From this cousin I heard that several members of the family were here today because they had lived 'underground' concealed by friends in the depths of the country. Husband and wife, brother and sister, had not seen each other for long periods, hidden in different places where at times they heard Gestapo men stamping outside, never sure when they would be discovered or caught.

After a few hours and having got over the nightmares of the

recent past, we became happier, able to recall memories of childhood and adolescence.

To reach Frankfurt in good time I had to leave the next day. There were then not many trains going into Germany, but I made efforts to find one to Detmold where I intended to make a short stop and visit my parents' graves. I succeeded in the end, and most appropriately, on a dark and miserable morning with the rain incessantly pouring from a leaden sky I passed the German frontier. There were many stops and it was late afternoon before I reached my hometown. In my hotel room, literally and perhaps hysterically, I wept myself to sleep. Next morning I went to the cemetery to find that my parents' graves had not been disturbed. On my walks I avoided Detmold's main street, not wanting to see our house or meet anybody I had known. However, in a small town nothing remains a secret for very long. As I sat down to lunch, the waiter handed me a note. It was from old neighbours who had somehow found out that I was there suggesting they collect me for a coffee and a chat.

In their company I did pass our house to discover that it was now a semi-ruin, one of the war's last casualties. We chatted for a couple of hours, talking about happy years and the sadness that was to follow. Nobody, they said, actually knew for certain what had happened to their Jewish fellow citizens. Certainly, they were 'taken away'. There were those who admitted to having seen them assembled in lorries in the market place. Beyond that there were only rumours and nobody had been able to get authentic news. Also, there had been a kind of mental block, made up of horror and fear, preventing people from enquiring. What was certain was that nobody had returned though there were now a few Jewish war refugees living in the town, apparently not mixing much with anybody. A long tradition of neighbourliness had been broken for ever.

A young woman, whose sister had been at school with me, recognised me and stopped to talk. Her family had for many years been neighbours of two maiden aunts of mine. They kept a *Pensionat* for young girls. Prim and proper, but generous and cheerful, they were well known and respected in the town, often seen taking their charges out on walks or to the theatre and concerts. Invitations to their parties were sought after, occasions in the social life of a small town. I had heard through the Red Cross that both aunts perished at Auschwitz. When I mentioned the fact to the girl, she appeared taken aback and said:

'Oh, we never knew what happened; we thought they had gone on a journey.'

She took a hurried farewell.

This insane response I found to be typical. It was perhaps a way of hiding from the facts by not acknowledging them.

From Detmold I took a train which, I was assured, would take me to Frankfurt where a hotel room was reserved for me. After several breakdowns on the main line – rolling stock was obviously in a poor state – we eventually reached Kassel at nightfall to be told that we could get no further that day. I was tired and cornered a porter to ask about accomodation. He shrugged his shoulders when I said, 'There is the *Nordische Hof* just outside the station, isn't there?'

With a wry smile he pulled me by the sleeve and out of the station entrance. 'There,' he said, pointing to miles and miles of rubble, looking ghostly in the bright light of the moon. 'That's your *Nordishe Hof* and the rest of it. But,' he continued, 'we deserved it, didn't we?' I was silent, but noticing my tiredness, he again pulled me by the sleeve, 'No need to despair, there is always the *Bunkerhotel.*' He then explained that outside Kassel's railway station there had been an air-raid shelter – *a Bunker* – now turned into a subterranean hotel. The porter showed me across the way and I walked into a cheerfully painted entrance hall.

At the reception it was confirmed that there would be an early morning train to Frankfurt and there was a room obtainable for the night. I was ushered into a pleasant little restaurant and served with strong coffee and open sandwiches which greatly helped to cheer me. Down several stairs my 'room' was a cubicle with just space enough to hold a bed. Washing facilities were available in a nearby bathroom. I undressed grateful to be able to lie down. However, in spite of tiredness and trying hard to rest, I could not sleep. I put my wakefulness down to the unpleasant noise from an air-conditioning system. But surely, this could not be the reason for the deep and frightening gloom which descended on me. By about three o'clock in the morning I could stand it no longer, got up, dressed and went to the restaurant which worked on a twenty-four hour basis.

The waiter who had served me in the evening was still on duty. Believing that I had made a mistake, he assured me that my train would not leave until seven o'clock. I explained why I had come to which he replied, 'I'll get you a good breakfast and then we will talk.' I was naturally the only guest at that time. The waiter asked to be allowed to sit down at my table and then under obvious stress he spoke of a heavy bombing attack on Kassel when part of the shelter had collapsed, burying many in the ruins. From those very ruins the *Bunkerhotel* was made. 'No wonder,' he added, 'you did not find rest in the place. I couldn't sleep here, and I never would.' A gruesome tale. I was glad when my train for Frankfurt arrived.

Much of Frankfurt was still in ruins but building appeared to be going on everywhere. My hotel was near the Book Fair and I spent all my time in that district, not having any great wish to go into a city which sadly lacked all its old landmarks and had no proper centre. The Fair itself was wonderful. Again I met a few, almost forgotten, old friends and made new ones. Also, I did more successful work for my Foreign Department in a few days than I would have done by writing dozens of letters. The old-established firm of wholesale booksellers, Köhler and Volckmar, had left Leipzig, now in the Russian zone, for Stuttgart, and to Stuttgart I had to travel to do some business with them.

I was welcomed as a customer and taken to the large stockrooms where I picked up several piles of books and was then invited to lunch by one of the men in charge. We spent a pleasant hour 'talking books' before the end of the meal when my host remarked quite innocently, 'Sorry, Madam, for the simple fare. It's all we have to offer just now. It would, of course, have been different had our *Führer* won the war.' Holding myself in tightly, I made no reply, but found it necessary to leave for the station at once. After a short, relaxing break at Strasbourg, a city I have always loved, it was to be Paris with another round of publishers.

As a member of P.E.N. I had been fortunate in obtaining a room in their Paris residential club. I was greeted by an elderly Yugoslav housekeeper whose French was very basic. Knowing that I came from Scotland, she tried to tell me that a '*fameux Ecossais*' was occupying the room next to mine. All I was to know about my neighbour that night, was that he snored heavily. Picture my pleasure next morning when over breakfast he turned out to be none other than Compton Mackenzie, in Paris for the opening of the French version of *Whisky Galore*. As I was to dine with a publisher that night, I could not accept Compton's kind invitation to see the film. However, together with the publisher, I took part in the reception which followed and it made a cheerful ending to a journey I had dreaded.

On this very journey, in the train between Frankfurt and Stuttgart, I suddenly discovered that my horror at being in Germany had vanished. I looked at the passing scene as if I were looking at a foreign country, with the eyes of a tourist.

The umbilical cord had been cut and it was a good thing.

During all my years in Scotland I counted many men amongst my friends, never believing for a moment that friendship between man and woman is impossible. I worked beside men and found them good companions in many of my leisure activities. I never 'suffered' from being a woman nor did I feel inferior or discriminated against. True, I sometimes had to stand up for getting the same pay as men, but my responsibilities were never different from those of a man. Perhaps through my early disappointment with romantic love, also through being in a new country and unsure of myself at a critical age, I had never allowed myself to become emotionally involved. In my generation it was usually a choice between marriage and a career, the two not being accepted simultaneously. Work meant a lot to me at all times and to give it up, and my independence, never seemed quite worth it. Indeed, work filled my life to the point where I would not lightly exchange it for any lasting relationship.

Then, one evening towards the end of the war, I was making my cumbersome way throught the black-out to one of those small 'utility' parties where the hostess proudly supplied coffee and everybody was to bring their own sandwich or biscuits while talk went on endlessly. I had been reluctant to accept this particular invitation as I was on fire-watching duty later that night. However, I was persuaded to go, if only for a short time. As I entered the dimly-lit drawing room, filled with the clinking of coffee cups and chatting people, I was suddenly aware of a voice, coming from a window seat. The voice drew me irresistibly towards it. It came from a man I had never seen before, yet we began talking at once about everything under the sun, both of us bubbling over, trying to get a word in. We eventually parted having hardly taken notice of anybody else present. We exchanged addresses, knowing that before long we should want to continue talking. Our next meeting came quite soon and many more followed. In the course of one of them my new friend told me that on the night of the party he had willed me to come across to him the moment he heard me greeting our hostess.

The spark which kindled love at first sight between my parents so many years ago, had worked again.

We were married in 1952.

And now, thirty years later, I am alone again. But there is no question of identity. I am completely at home in my new country and particularly so in that tiny piece of Scotland which is my own and the garden I cultivate there. My memories remain with me, the happy ones and the sad, and above all the bright kaleidoscope of my childhood.